First World War
and Army of Occupation
War Diary
France, Belgium and Germany

40 DIVISION
Divisional Troops
Royal Army Medical Corps
137 Field Ambulance
2 June 1916 - 31 May 1919

WO95/2602/3

The Naval & Military Press Ltd
www.nmarchive.com
Published in association with The National Archives

Published by

The Naval & Military Press Ltd

Unit 10 Ridgewood Industrial Park,

Uckfield, East Sussex,

TN22 5QE England

Tel: +44 (0) 1825 749494

www.naval-military-press.com

www.nmarchive.com

This diary has been reprinted in facsimile from the original. Any imperfections are inevitably reproduced and the quality may fall short of modern type and cartographic standards.

© **Crown Copyright**
Images reproduced by permission of The National Archives, London, England, 2015.

Contents

Document type	Place/Title	Date From	Date To
Heading	WO95/2602/3		
Heading	40th Division 137th Field Ambulance Jun 1916-1919 May		
Heading	June 1916. No. 137 F.a.		
War Diary	Bullswater Camp.	02/06/1916	02/06/1916
War Diary	Pirbright	02/06/1916	02/06/1916
War Diary	Farnborough Station	03/06/1916	03/06/1916
War Diary	Southampton	03/06/1916	03/06/1916
War Diary	Le Havre	04/06/1916	05/06/1916
War Diary	Monterolier Buchy	05/06/1916	06/06/1916
War Diary	Abbeville	06/06/1916	06/06/1916
War Diary	Lillers	06/06/1916	06/06/1916
War Diary	Fontes	06/06/1916	11/06/1916
War Diary	Ruitz	20/06/1916	30/06/1916
Heading	Medical Services War Diary. of O.C. 137th Fd: Ambulance. for month of July 1916. (Volume 2.)		
War Diary	Ruitz	01/07/1916	03/07/1916
War Diary	Bracquemont	03/07/1916	31/07/1916
Miscellaneous	40th Div 137th Field Ambulance. August 1916		
War Diary	Braquemont (36B.L25.b 2.5.)	01/08/1916	07/08/1916
War Diary	Braquemont	07/08/1916	31/08/1916
Miscellaneous	40th Div. 137th. Field Ambulance Sept. 1916		
War Diary	Braquemont. L25.b 2.5.	01/09/1916	07/09/1916
War Diary	Braquemont	08/09/1916	30/09/1916
Miscellaneous	40th Div 137th. Field Ambulance Oct 1916		
War Diary	Braquemont (36B 1/40,000) L25.b2.5.	01/10/1916	05/10/1916
War Diary	Braquemont	05/10/1916	11/10/1916
War Diary	Labeuvriere (36B.) D17 a 4.5.	12/10/1916	12/10/1916
War Diary	Labeuvriere	12/10/1916	29/10/1916
War Diary	Bruay J 16 c 2.0. (36 B 1/40,000)	30/10/1916	30/10/1916
War Diary	Guestreville V 13 C 1.5. (36 B 1/40,000)	31/10/1916	31/10/1916
Miscellaneous	40th Div 137th. Field Ambulance Nov. 1916		
War Diary	Guestreville 36 B 1/40,000 V 13. C 1.5.	01/11/1916	02/11/1916
War Diary	Oppy Lens Sheet, 1/100,000 E 3.16.24.	02/11/1916	04/11/1916
War Diary	Outrebois Lens Sheet, 1/100,000 D 4.15.5.10.8.	04/11/1916	04/11/1916
War Diary	Outre Bois Gorges Lens Sheet, 1/100,000. C 5.10.8.6.8.	05/11/1916	13/11/1916
War Diary	Gorges	14/11/1916	15/11/1916
War Diary	Mezerolles	15/11/1916	17/11/1916
War Diary	Bouquemaison	17/11/1917	18/11/1917
War Diary	Warluzel	18/11/1917	22/11/1917
War Diary	Bretel	22/11/1917	23/11/1917
War Diary	Pernois	23/11/1917	24/11/1917
War Diary	Pont Remy	24/11/1917	26/11/1917
War Diary	L'Etoile	26/11/1917	30/11/1917
Miscellaneous	40th Div. 137th Field Ambulance Dec. 1916		
War Diary	L'Etoile. (Lens Sheet' No.11 1/100,000)	01/12/1916	08/12/1916
War Diary	L'Etoile	08/12/1916	11/12/1916
War Diary	Sailly-Laurette	11/12/1916	27/12/1916
War Diary	Suzanne	27/12/1916	31/12/1916
Miscellaneous	40th Div 137th. Field Ambulance. Jan. 1917/S		

Type	Description	From	To
War Diary	Camp 17 Near Suzanne (Albert Sheet 1/40,000 G 8 b 5.7.)	01/01/1917	10/01/1917
War Diary	Camp 17.	11/01/1917	31/01/1917
Miscellaneous	40th Div. 137th Field Ambulance. Feb. 1917/S		
War Diary	Camp 12 (Chipilly)	01/02/1917	10/02/1917
War Diary	Bray (Albert Sheet 1/40,000 L15.d.5.7.)	11/02/1917	14/02/1917
War Diary	Bray	15/02/1917	28/02/1917
Miscellaneous	137th. f.a. mar 1917 /S		
War Diary	Bray L 15. d 5.9. (Albert Sheet 1/40,000)	01/03/1917	05/03/1917
War Diary	Bray	05/03/1917	09/03/1917
War Diary	Hem (Albert Sheet 1/40,000 H 8 a. 2.7.)	09/03/1917	20/03/1917
War Diary	Clery Sheet 62 c (H 6 c 9.5.)	20/03/1917	25/03/1917
War Diary	Clery	25/03/1917	25/03/1917
War Diary	Maurepas Camp 163 63 c 1/40,000 B14c. (Central)	26/03/1917	31/03/1917
Miscellaneous	137th f.a. April 1917		
War Diary	Camp 163 (Sheet 62 c b14.c. Central	01/04/1917	04/04/1917
War Diary	Camp 163	04/04/1917	07/04/1917
War Diary	Moislains Sheet 62 c (1/40,000) C 12 c.7.7.	07/04/1917	08/04/1917
War Diary	Moislains	14/04/1917	23/04/1917
War Diary	Manancourt (57 c 1/40,000) V13a.9.4.	23/04/1917	23/04/1917
War Diary	Manancourt	23/04/1917	30/04/1917
Miscellaneous	40th Div. No.137. f.a. may 1917		
War Diary	Manancourt (Sheet 57 c 1/40,000 V 13.a.9.4.)	01/05/1917	04/05/1917
War Diary	Manancourt	05/05/1917	14/05/1917
War Diary	Heudicourt (Sheet 57 c 1/40,000 N 21b.3.9.)	14/05/1917	18/05/1917
War Diary	Heudicourt	19/05/1917	23/05/1917
War Diary	Manancourt V 13 a 9.4. (Sheet 57 C)	23/05/1917	24/05/1917
War Diary	Manancourt	25/05/1917	31/05/1917
Miscellaneous	Scheme of Evacuation from Right Brigade Appendix I	16/05/1917	16/05/1917
Miscellaneous	No. 137. F.A. June 1917.		
War Diary	Manancourt (Sheet 57 c 1/40,000 V 13.a.9.4.)	01/06/1917	07/06/1917
War Diary	Manancourt	08/06/1917	30/06/1917
Miscellaneous	No. 137. F.A. July. 1917.		
War Diary	Manancourt (Sheet 57 c 1/40,000 V 13.a.9.4)	02/07/1917	03/07/1917
War Diary	Heudicourt (Sheet 57 c 1/40,000. W 21b3.9.)	03/07/1917	06/07/1917
War Diary	Heudicourt	07/07/1917	31/07/1917
Miscellaneous	Scheme of Evacuation from Right Brigade Appendix I	03/07/1917	03/07/1917
Miscellaneous	Alteration in the Position of the R.A.Ps Appendix. 2.		
Miscellaneous	Appendix 3.	31/07/1917	31/07/1917
Miscellaneous	No. 137. F.A. Aug. 1917.		
War Diary	Heudicourt (Sheet 57 c 1/40,000 W 21. b. 39.)	01/08/1917	02/08/1917
War Diary	Heudicourt	02/08/1917	21/08/1917
War Diary	Fins (V 18. c.)	22/08/1917	31/08/1917
Miscellaneous	Appendix. To August Diary. Appendix. I.	02/08/1917	02/08/1917
Miscellaneous	No. 137 F.A. Sept. 1917		
War Diary	Fins (Sheet 57 C V 18 C.)	03/09/1917	17/09/1917
War Diary	Fins	19/09/1917	30/09/1917
Miscellaneous	Reference.-Sheet 57 C S.E. 1/20,000 System of Evacuation of Casualties night of 25/26th Sept.17	25/09/1917	25/09/1917
Miscellaneous	No. 137. F.A. Oct. 1917		
War Diary	Fins (Sheet 57 C 1/40,000 V 18 c.)	02/10/1917	07/10/1917
War Diary	Fins (V 18c)	07/10/1917	10/10/1917
War Diary	Peronne Sheet 62 c 1/40,000 I.27 b.	10/10/1917	12/10/1917
War Diary	Barly. Sheet 51 c 1/40,000 P 15.d.2.7.	13/10/1917	14/10/1917
War Diary	Barly.	21/10/1917	29/10/1917
War Diary	Warluzel (Sheet 51 c 1/40,000 O.27 a.8.9.)	29/10/1917	31/10/1917

Miscellaneous	No. 137. F.A. Nov. 1917.		
War Diary	Warluzel (Sheet 51 c 1/40,000 O 27 c 8.9.)	01/11/1917	16/11/1917
War Diary	Barly 51 c 1/40,000 p 15 d 2.7.	16/11/1917	17/11/1917
War Diary	Achiet-Le-Grand Sheet 57 c 1/40,000 G 9.b.4.6.	18/11/1917	18/11/1917
War Diary	Achiet-Le-Grand	18/11/1917	19/11/1917
War Diary	Rocquigny (Sheet 57 C 1/40,000 O 27d.6.9.)	20/11/1917	20/11/1917
War Diary	Rocquigny.	20/11/1917	21/11/1917
War Diary	Beaumetz-Les-Cambrai	21/11/1917	22/11/1917
War Diary	Demicourt	22/11/1917	23/11/1917
War Diary	Bertincourt	27/11/1917	27/11/1917
War Diary	Beaumetz Les Loges	27/11/1917	27/11/1917
War Diary	Bailleulmont	27/11/1917	30/11/1917
Miscellaneous	Medical Arrangements in forward area, during operations of 40th Division, Period Nov 22nd to Nov 26th, 1917 Inclusive.	22/11/1917	22/11/1917
Miscellaneous	No. 137. F.A. Dec. 1917		
War Diary	Lens Sheet 1/100000 Bailleulmont	01/12/1917	01/12/1917
War Diary	Hamelincourt	01/12/1917	01/12/1917
War Diary	Ervillers 57 c 1/40,000 B 13 d 2.2.	01/12/1917	02/12/1917
War Diary	57 c 1/4000 B 13 d 2.2. Ervillers	02/12/1917	11/12/1917
War Diary	Sheet 57 c 1/40000 B 13 d 22 Ervillers	12/12/1917	14/12/1917
War Diary	Sheet 57 c 1/40000 A 5 a 8.4 Hamelincourt	15/12/1917	26/12/1917
War Diary	Hamelincourt	28/12/1917	29/12/1917
War Diary	Ervillers Sheet 57 c 1/40000 B 13 d. 2.5	29/12/1917	29/12/1917
Miscellaneous	No. 137. F.A. Jan. 1918.		
War Diary	Ervillers (Sh 57 c 1/40,000 b 13 d 2.2)	01/01/1918	24/01/1918
War Diary	Ervillers	25/01/1918	31/01/1918
Miscellaneous	Appendix A.		
Miscellaneous	No. 137. F.A. Feb. 1918.		
War Diary	Ervillers (Sht 57 c 1/40000 B 13 d 22)	01/02/1918	12/02/1918
War Diary	Durham Lines A (Sh 51 b 1/40000 S11 a 36)	13/02/1918	20/02/1918
War Diary	Durham Lines A.	21/02/1918	28/02/1918
Miscellaneous	Appendix A.		
Miscellaneous			
Heading	No. 137 Field Ambulance medical Card.		
Miscellaneous	137th. Field Ambulance. mar. 1918.		
War Diary	Bailleulmont	01/03/1918	11/03/1918
War Diary	Durham Lines Sh. 51 B 1/40,000 S 11 a 36.	12/03/1918	22/03/1918
War Diary	Armagh Camp S23 a 11 (Sh. 5 1 B 1/40000 Ayette)	22/03/1918	24/03/1918
War Diary	Bucquoy	24/03/1918	25/03/1918
War Diary	Monchy-Au Bois	26/03/1918	26/03/1918
War Diary	Pommier	26/03/1918	26/03/1918
War Diary	Noyellette	27/03/1918	27/03/1918
War Diary	Sus St Leger	27/03/1918	28/03/1918
War Diary	Orlencourt	29/03/1918	30/03/1918
War Diary	Doulieu	31/03/1918	31/03/1918
Miscellaneous	137th. Field Ambulance. apr. 1918.		
War Diary	Fort Rompu (H 7 d 73 Sh 36)	01/04/1918	09/04/1918
War Diary	Vieux Berquin	10/04/1918	11/04/1918
War Diary	Pradelles	12/04/1918	13/04/1918
War Diary	Zuytpeene	13/04/1918	13/04/1918
War Diary	Scaderburg (St Omer)	14/04/1918	20/04/1918
War Diary	(N 24 a Sh. 27)	21/04/1918	22/04/1918
War Diary	(J 15 d 05 Sh 27)	23/04/1918	27/04/1918
War Diary	Mendinghem	28/04/1918	30/04/1918
Miscellaneous	Appendix.		

Miscellaneous	No. 137 F.A. May 1918.		
War Diary	Mendinghem (Sh. 27 E 6 d 55)	01/05/1918	02/05/1918
War Diary	J 15 d 05 (Sh 27)	03/05/1918	03/05/1918
War Diary	Kinderbelck. (Hazebrouck 5A).	04/05/1918	09/05/1918
War Diary	Kinderbelck	10/05/1918	31/05/1918
Miscellaneous	No. 137 F.A. June 1918		
War Diary	Kinderbelck (Sh 27 1/40000 G 33 c 88.)	01/06/1918	22/06/1918
War Diary	C 8 b 57 (Sheet 36 A)	23/06/1918	28/06/1918
War Diary	T 22 a 3.4. (Sh 27)	29/06/1918	30/06/1918
Miscellaneous	Appendix 137 Field Ambulance		
Miscellaneous	137 F. F.A. July 1918.		
War Diary	T 22. a. 3.4. (Sh 27)	01/07/1918	31/07/1918
Miscellaneous	137 Field Ambulance Appendix		
Miscellaneous	137. f.a. aug. 1918.		
War Diary	Sheet 27 1/40000 T 22 a. 3.4	01/08/1918	23/08/1918
War Diary	36A/C5a59	24/08/1918	31/08/1918
Miscellaneous	137th field amb. Sept. 1918		
War Diary	La Motte (36 A/D 30 d 09)	01/09/1918	07/09/1918
War Diary	36/A 21 b 28	08/09/1918	30/09/1918
Miscellaneous	Appendix 137 Field Amb.		
Miscellaneous	137th f.a. Oct 1918		
War Diary	La Briele Farm 36 A L 5 a 60	01/10/1918	01/10/1918
War Diary	Steenwercke Chateau	02/10/1918	17/10/1918
War Diary	Wambrechies	18/10/1918	31/10/1918
Miscellaneous	Appendix 137 Field Ambulance		
Miscellaneous	137th. f.a. Nov. 1918.		
War Diary	Wambrechies	01/11/1918	02/11/1918
War Diary	Chateau	02/11/1918	02/11/1918
War Diary	Lionderie.	03/11/1918	08/11/1918
War Diary	Pecq	09/11/1918	15/11/1918
War Diary	Croix (Roubaix)	16/11/1918	30/11/1918
Miscellaneous	Appendix. 137 Field Ambulance.		
Miscellaneous	No. 137. F.A. Dec. 1918		
War Diary	Croix (nr. Roubaix)	01/12/1918	20/12/1918
War Diary	Croix	21/12/1918	28/12/1918
Miscellaneous	137 Field Ambulance Appendix		
Miscellaneous	40 Div Box 2418 no. 137 f.a Jan 1919		
War Diary	Croix (Nr Roubaix)	01/01/1919	31/01/1919
Miscellaneous	No. 137 Field Ambulance Feb. 1919		
War Diary	Croix (near Roubaix)	01/02/1919	28/02/1919
Miscellaneous	Appendix 137 Field Ambulance		
Miscellaneous	137th f.a. mar. 1919		
War Diary	Croix (nr) Roubaix	01/03/1919	31/03/1919
Miscellaneous	137th f.a. apr. 1919		
War Diary	Croix near Roubaix	01/04/1919	30/04/1919
Miscellaneous	No. 137 Field Ambulance. May, 1919		
War Diary	Croix Nr Roubaix	01/05/1919	31/05/1919

W045/2092/3

40TH DIVISION

137TH FIELD AMBULANCE
JUN 1916 - ~~DEC 1918~~ 1919 MAY

40TH DIVISION

CMO. 137 17.a.

June 1915.

COMMITTEE FOR THE
MEDICAL HISTORY OF THE WAR
Date 5 AUG. 1915

Army Form C. 2118.

Vol 1

137th Field Ambulance
R.A.M.C.
June

WAR DIARY
or
INTELLIGENCE SUMMARY
(Erase heading not required.)

Instructions regarding War Diaries and Intelligence Summaries are contained in F.S. Regs., Part II. and the Staff Manual respectively. Title Pages will be prepared in manuscript.

Place	Date 1916	Hour	Summary of Events and Information	Remarks and references to Appendices
BULLSWATER CAMP. PIRBRIGHT	2nd June	11 P.M.	Unit moved out of camp for entrainment at FARNBOROUGH STATION (L.S.W.R.)	
FARNBOROUGH STATION	3rd June	3.30 AM	Unit arrived. Men, horses and vehicles entrained and ready to move off at 4.10 A.M. Train left station at 4.20 o'clock. Strength of unit :— 11 Officers (including 2 Chaplains attached), 2 N.O's (include. ASC?) 219 N.C.O.s and men including A.S.C., 3'5" Horses and Mules (shortage of 1 Riding Horse), 14 four-wheeled and 4 two-wheeled vehicles.	
SOUTHAMPTON DOCKS	3rd June	6 A.M.	Unit arrived at SOUTHAMPTON DOCKS. Embarked on Transport AFRICAN PRINCE at 8.30 P.M. Sailed at 6 P.M.	
LE HAVRE	4th June	4 A.M.	Transport arrived at HAVRE after good voyage. No casualties. Disembarked at 10 hours. Unshipped animals (M.S.) and vehicles by 12 hours. Arrived Rest Camp No. 2 at 14.30 hours.	
"	4th June	17.40 hours	Received orders to entrain at HAVRE STATION at 12 hours 5th June.	
"	5th June	10 hours	Unit left Camp No. 2 for railway station. Arrived at station 11.30. Train departed 15 hours. During the journey one officer's cob was obtained from Remount Dept & rails up shortage which had existed since departure from BULLSWATER. Two heavy charger? horses were exchanged at this Dept, also.	
MONTÉROLIER BUCHY	5th June	20.30 hours	Train arrived MONTÉROLIER BUCHY. Hot meals was obtained. Animals watered. Men received Rations of stew.	
ABBEVILLE	6th June	3.25	Train arrived. Hot water obtained. Men warmed with tea and rations for the day. Train departed to time.	
LILLERS	6th June	9.15	Train arrived. Heavy rain. Animals and vehicles detrained without delay. Unit moved off & its billeting area at 11 hours. The officer who had preceded the unit to FRANCE met it on arrival at LILLERS and acted as guide to the billeting area.	
FONTES	6th June	12,30	Field Ambulance arrived at its billeting area - men distributed without delay. Section Pell intact as far as possible. Unit on both sides of the main road. Horses picketed in a field off main road - whilst parked in same place.	

2449 Wt. W14957/M90 750,000 1/16 J.B.C. & A. Forms/C.2118/12.

WAR DIARY or INTELLIGENCE SUMMARY

Army Form C. 2118.

137th Field Ambulance
R A M C

Place	Date	Hour	Summary of Events and Information	Remarks and references to Appendices
FONTES	June 8	17 hrs 25	Order received from A.D.M.S. to detail 2 Horsed Ambulance Wagons to march behind 119th R.W.F. and 17th Welsh Regiment. Proceeding tomorrow to the front. Two days rations for horses and men in the station. The Ambulance Wagons to return when the N.C.O. rated units have arrived at the front. Timbs and Lightbody detailed by S.O.1.	
		17 hrs 40	Order received from S.O.1. Two ambulance wagons to be accompanying 119th Inf. Bde. forming Rear Battalion dined to pass BOURECQ Church 9 A.M. Route — LILLIERS — ALLOUAGNE — MARLES LES MINES — HAILLICOURT — HOUCHIN — ?	
	9	8 hrs	Ambulance wagons under Capt. A.J. BEVERIDGE as guide, departed for church BOURECQ. A corporal and 4 privates R.A.M.C. detailed to accompany them as wagon orderlies.	
		15 hrs 30	Orders received from A.D.M.S. to proceed with 'A' Section of the Fd. Amb. to NOEUX-LES-MINES. That 36 B / 40,000th K.I.D.C. on the 11th inst. The town of move ½ to occupied by one. To report arrival to A.D.M.S. 16th Division. Map hearing as above. To take two motor ambulance wagons, and riding horses, no other equipment. To take one days rations in a stuff cart, plus centralized pouches. Quartermaster not to proceed. The section will proceed to divided between the Field Ambulances when it arrives.	
		16 hrs 50	In continuation of above, orders received of personnel and horses probable hour of arrival, strength of personnel and horses.	
	10	15 hrs	G.O.C. Division visited Field Ambulance.	
	11	8 hrs	'A' Section of the Fd. Amb. LW, by march order, for NOEUX-LES-MINES.	
		15 hrs	Letter arrived. 'A' NOEUX-LES-MINES. Officer starting arrival L' A.D.M.S. 16th Division. The Section proceeded to main dressing station of 113th Fd. Amb.	
		19 hrs	Officer Co. detail 'A' Section proceeded to advanced dressing station at PHILOSOPHE and LOOS.	

Army Form C. 2118.

WAR DIARY
or
INTELLIGENCE SUMMARY

137th Field Ambulance
R.A.M.C.

(Erase heading not required.)

Instructions regarding War Diaries and Intelligence Summaries are contained in F. S. Regs., Part II. and the Staff Manual respectively. Title Pages will be prepared in manuscript.

Place	Date	Hour	Summary of Events and Information	Remarks and references to Appendices
RUITZ	20th	15 hrs	'A' Section returned from NOEUX-LES-MINES Bearer undergoes 10 days Training with 113 F.A. and already united at advanced dressing stations to LOOS and became affiliated with corps work in the trenches. During the absence of the O.C. unit with "A" Section, orders were received by officer in temporary command of unit viz 'A' Section, to leave FONTES to RUITZ. Orders received at midnight 16/17 - unit moved out from FONTES at 3.45. 19 inst. arrived at RUITZ 11.35 hrs. same day.	NIL
	21st	16.30	"B" Section with 3 officers, 60 N.C.O's & men, 1 Leslant-mgm, 2 motor ambulance cars proceeded by road route 'b' to NOEUX-LES-MINES to & annex of dressing station at RUITZ for deep of 112th Field Ambulance. "A" Section opened up dressing station at RUITZ for deep of 121st Inf. Bde. and attached at BARLIN. "C" Section in reserve.	NIL
			Admissions O.R. 1 Sick	Admissions O.R. 2 Sick NIL
	22nd	15'	Attended conference at Office A.D.M.S.	NIL
	23rd		Admissions O.R. 1 Sick.	NIL
	24th		Admissions O.R. 1 Sick	NIL
	25th		Admissions O.R. 1 Sick	NIL
	26th		Admissions O.R. 1 Sick	NIL
	27th		Admissions Officer 1 O.R. 3 Sick	NIL

Army Form C. 2118.

WAR DIARY
or
INTELLIGENCE SUMMARY 137th Field Ambulance
R.A.M.C.

(Erase heading not required.)

Instructions regarding War Diaries and Intelligence Summaries are contained in F. S. Regs., Part II. and the Staff Manual respectively. Title Pages will be prepared in manuscript.

Place	Date	Hour	Summary of Events and Information	Remarks and references to Appendices
RUITZ	28		Admission Officer 1. O.R. 1. Sur Nil.	A
"	29		Admission O.R. 1. Sur Nil	
"	30		Admission O.R. 2. Sur Nil. During the past week the personnel of the unit has been receiving instruction in the wearing of P.H. Helmets. Lectures and practical work in First Aid.	

[signature]
MAJOR R.A.M.C.
COMMANDING 137 FIELD AMBULANCE.

Confidential.

Medical Services.

War Diary.

of

O.C. 137th Fd: Ambulance.

for

Month of July, 1916.

(Volume 2.)

SECRET.

WAR DIARY Vol IT
or
INTELLIGENCE SUMMARY

Army Form C. 2118.

137½ Field Ambulance
R.A.M.C.

(Erase heading not required.)

Instructions regarding War Diaries and Intelligence Summaries are contained in F. S. Regs., Part II. and the Staff Manual respectively. Title Pages will be prepared in manuscript.

Place	Date	Hour	Summary of Events and Information	Remarks and references to Appendices
RUITZ	July 1	17 hrs	"B" Section returned from 112th Fd. Amb. NOEUX-LES-MINES at 19 hrs. 30.6.16.	
"	"		"C" Section left for instruction with 112th Fd. Amb. NOEUX-LES-MINES. Strength: 1 Officer, 2 Staff Sergts R.A.M.C. 3/9 A.S.C. 9. 1 horsed wagon, 3 motor ambulance cars, 2 Motor lorries. Admin: 1 Officer, 2 Other Ranks. AW	
"	2	19 hrs	Orders received from A.D.M.S. H.Q. Division to proceed in 2 Fd. Amb. cars to NOEUX-LES-MINES early to' morrow with O.C. No.1 Fd. Amb. to 1st H.Q. Station over 3rd Advanced Mair dressing Station Stores etc: To move in with complete unit on the unit: All sick at "special" in Fd. Amb. Lily evacuated L 2 C.C.S. D Rly Station to duty. AW	
"	3	1 hr.	Received from 121st Infantry Brigade orders to L' nor of Brigade L' Rly Mr front of the Rd. by 1st Division. Proceeded at 8 hs 30. to NOEUX-LES-MINES (BRAQUEMONT) 368, L23/82.3.1 and interviewed O.C. No.1 Fd. Amb. Inspected Main Railway Station and then proceeded to Advanced Dsing Station at LES BREBIS, NORTH and SOUTH MARIE Pit Groups 36 B. L33'.A.8.3., 36 C M2d47., 36 C M3f1.4. Inspected Mineral Baths and Staff Kitchen at LES BREBIS. Returned to unit at RUITZ at 13 hrs. Handed over unit from RUITZ to BRACQUEMONT at 14 hrs. 30.- Detail of BRACQUEMONT and Troops from O.C. 1 Fd. Amb.	
BRACQUEMONT	3	16 hrs	Arrived with unit, less "C" Section, at BRACQUEMONT and took over from O.C. 1 Fd. Amb.	

2449 Wt. W14957/M90 750,000 1/16 J.B.C. & A. Forms/C.2118/12.

WAR DIARY
or
INTELLIGENCE SUMMARY

(Erase heading not required.)

Army Form C. 2118.

Vol II.

Place	Date	Hour	Summary of Events and Information	Remarks and references to Appendices
BRACQUEMONT	July 3	18 hrs.	3 Officers, 9 N.C.O's, 63 privates, 4 Motor Ambulance Cars, horse transport of "A" Section both linked wagons, proceeded to' LES BREBIS to take over duties of 113th Field Amb and of NORTHAM SOUTH MARSH. "C" Section returned from 112th Fd. Amb. This section together with details from 'B' section posted to duties at MAIN DRESSING STATION. Admissions O.R. 9, wounded; 13 starred, sick. A.I.	
"	4		Admissions O.R. 30, sick; 5 wounded. Took over Divisional Baths and Workshops at LES BREBIS. A.I.	
"	5		Admissions: Other ranks sick 2, O.R. 17 sick/wounded. A.I.	
"	6		470 men put through Divisional Baths between hours of 8.30 and 12.30. Admissions: Sick – Officers 2, O.R. 19 A.I. Wounded " 0, O.R. 7	
"	7		Admissions Sick O.R. 13 A.I. Wounded O.R. 17	
"	8		Received two privates as reinforcements from No 5' General Base Depot". Admissions: Sick O.R. 25 A.I. Wounded O.R. 3	
"	9		LIEUT. H.L. McCORMICK returned to the unit for duty from 40th Divisional Laundry. Admissions: Sick O.R. 15' A.I. Wounded officer 1, O.R. 13. A.I.	

WAR DIARY or INTELLIGENCE SUMMARY

Army Form C. 2118.
Vol II.

(Erase heading not required.)

Place	Date	Hour	Summary of Events and Information	Remarks and references to Appendices
BRAQUEMNT	July 10		Sergeant Major P. MEEHAN of this Unit evacuated sick to No. 1 C.C.S. — AJ Admissions sick O.R. 11 Wounded O.R. 3	
"	11		Admissions Officer sick 1 O.R. sick 14 O.R. wounded 4 AJ	
"	12		Admissions Officer sick 1 O.R. sick 15 O.R. wounded 7 AJ	
"	13		Admissions sick O.R. 9 wounded O.R. 2 AJ	
"	14		Admissions sick O.R. 18 wounded O.R. 4 AJ	
"	15	13hrs 30	Visited LES BREBIS and SOUTH MAROC L'ecorme Trench Railway Tramway between these places - H' ascertain whether it is suitable for transport of wounded. Narrow gauge with wheels adapted for carriage of stretchers in two tiers - capacity 4 lying down cases each truck. In all about 25' lying down cases can be carried each journey. The line is laid Trench level and the method of transport is low in use by night; it is from -Sett-fontaine rendez... The train is shown by small motor engine and is also used on the upward journey for the conveyance of R.E. stores, supplies etc. 2' mile N. Noir and South MAROC. Admissions sick O.R. 23 wounded O.R. 7. AJ	
"	16	12noon	"C" Section 136 FIELD AMBULANCE arrived from LABEUVRIERE to temporary duty with this Unit. The transfer accompanying the section returned h' Headquarters of 136 FD. AMB. as the is with ascertation no use for it Lee. The section is	

WAR DIARY or INTELLIGENCE SUMMARY

Army Form C. 2118. Vol. II.

Place	Date	Hour	Summary of Events and Information	Remarks and references to Appendices
BRAQUEMONT	July 16		Distributed as follows:— 1 Officer 23 O.R. to Main Nursing Station, BRAQUEMONT:— 1 Officer 20 Q.R.L. Advanced Nursing Station No 2. LES BREBIS — 1 Officer 12 O.R.L. SOUTH MAROC (Advanced Nursing Station No 1). Nursing orderlies, cooks, clerks etc. all allocated to their own particular duties as far as possible. Admissions O.R. sick 7. O.R. wounded 2.	
"	17		Admissions Officer sick 1. O.R. sick 20 wounded 3. One corporal from 40th Divisional Supply Column joined unit as reinforcement — MJ	
"	18		Admissions Officers sick M) »»» 3 O.R. sick 22 wounded 5. W)	
"	19		Admissions Officers sick 1 O.R. sick 18 wounded 13. M)	
"	20		Admissions O.R. sick 9 wounded 4. Two reinforcements arrived from No 4 General Base, ROUEN — M)	
"	21		Admissions Officers sick 1 O.R. sick 16 wounded 11. W)	
"	"	14 hr 30	Received verbal instructions from A.D.M.S. 40th A Division to take over on 1/22 2/22 July the advanced dressing stations of the 113th Fd. Amb. 16th Division situated at PHILOSOPHE, St PATRICK'S and FORT GLATZ. The two latter being situated in LOOS. This was in relation of being shortly relieved by 40th Division. Following is distribution of personnel to these A. Dressing Stations:— 2 Officers and 32 Q.R. at PHILOSOPHE, 2 Officers 15 O.R. St. Patrick's and 70 O.R. at FORT GLATZ. Two motor ambulance cars and	

WAR DIARY or INTELLIGENCE SUMMARY

Army Form C. 2118.

W.H.I.

(Erase heading not required.)

Place	Date	Hour	Summary of Events and Information	Remarks and references to Appendices
BRAQUEMONT	July 21	22	On walk-out an MyDr permanent at PHILOSOPHE. On 21 hr 30 each night the additional ambulance cars leave headquarters in PHILOSOPHE. All the evacuation from LOOS is carried out during the night, to this extra two cars relieve up at PHILOSOPHE and for LOOP Posts LOOS and the Place, returning to Headquarters each morning and	
"	"		MAZINGARBE — NOEUX-LES-MINES. This relief was carried out in the night 21/22 at 22 hours. A nd. b' officer the relief of 113 Fd. Amb., No 3's but two was removed from Advanced Dressing Stations at NORTH and SOUTH MARIS and LES BREBIS, reducing the establishment of these stations to their original numbers.	NJ
"	22		Admission O.R. Dur 13 Wounded 13 1 O.R. R.A.M.C. evacuated to C.C.S.	NJ
"	23		Admissions Officers Sick 2 O.R. Sick 25 Wounded 12 3 days motor ambulance cars removed from 136 Fd. Amb. to augment existing establishment many to previous in units of advanced dressing stations.	NJ
"	24		Admissions Officers sick 1 O.R. sick 16 Wounded 19 3 two-wheeled stretcher carriages arrived from 136 Fd. Amb. L, augment existing established. The war sent to Advanced Dressing Stations 2, ST. PATRICKS and FORT GLATZ, Post at LOOS NW.	NJ
"	25		Admissions — Officers Sick 1 O.R. Sick 32 Wounded — Officers 1 O.R. 38	NJ
"	26		Admissions — Officers — Sick 1 O.R. Sick 21 O.R. Wounded 16	NJ
"	27		Admissions — Officers — Sick 1 O.R. Sick 18 O.R. Wounded 12 1 O.R. R.A.M.C. evacuated W.C.C.S. LIEUT. W.L. THOMAS, R.A.M.C. taken in its strength from No. 5 General Hospital	NJ

Army Form C. 2118.

Vol II.

WAR DIARY
or
INTELLIGENCE SUMMARY
(Erase heading not required.)

Place	Date	Hour	Summary of Events and Information	Remarks and references to Appendices
BRAQUEMONT	28		Admissions Officers Sick 2 O.R. Sick 15. Wounded — Officers 1 O.R. 32. The complete staff at NORTH and SOUTH MAROC advanced dressing stations were relieved by personnel from Advanced Dressing Station LES BREBIS. First half of relief, 5 Officers and other ranks being detached in LOOS sector sent up from Headquarters — this consisted of 1 N.C.O. 22 Men. also 1 Officer. LIEUT. CRAIG. R.M 136th F.D. AMB. attached 137th F.D. AMB. posted as M.O. I/c 12th YORKS. REGT. permanently. AW.	
"	29		Admissions Officers Sick 1. O.R. Sick 23. Officers Wound 1. O.R. wounded 18 AW	
"	30		Admissions O.R. Sick 10. O.R. Wounded 49 AW	
"	31		Admissions Officers Sick 1 O.R. Sick 19. Wounded 26 AW	
"		14 hrs 30	Attended conference of Officer A.D.M.S. 46th Division	

[signature]
LIEUT. COLONEL, R.A.M.C.
COMMANDING 187 FIELD AMBULANCE.

Auqhigh
H.O.T. 10W
137th Field Ambulance

COMMITTEE FOR THE
MEDICAL HISTORY OF THE WAR
Date -9 OCT 1916

SECRET.

Army Form C.² 2118.

Instructions regarding War Diaries and Intelligence Summaries are contained in F.S. Regs., Part II. and the Staff Manual respectively. Title Pages will be prepared in manuscript.

WAR DIARY or INTELLIGENCE SUMMARY

(Erase heading not required.)

137th Field Ambulance,
Volume III
R.A.M.C.

Place	Date	Hour	Summary of Events and Information	Remarks and references to Appendices
BRAQUEMONT (36.B.L.25.b.2.3)	August 1916 1		Admissions. Officers – Nil. Other ranks – Nil. Sick 14. Wounded 9. (A)	
	2		Returned two heavy Mtr Ambulance Cars with 3 O.R's A.S.C. M.T., to 136th Field Ambulance. Admissions. Other ranks – Sick 34. Wounded 24. Officers – wounded 1. (A)	
	3		Admissions. Officers – Sick 2. Other ranks – Sick 25. Wounded 29. (A)	
	4		Admissions. Officers – Sick 2. Other ranks – Sick 13. Wounded 13. Officers relieved 21st Advanced Dressing Stations – A general re-distribution. (A)	
	5		Admissions. Other ranks – Sick 15. Wounded 8. Attended conference at office A.D.M.S. 40th Division.	
		14h.30m		
		12 hrs	Personnel at LOOS and PHILOSOPHE Advanced Dressing Stations relieved by N.C.O's and men from Dressing Station, BRAQUEMONT.	
	6		Admissions. Officers – Sick 1. Other ranks – Sick 12. Wounded 12. (A)	
	7		Admissions. O.R. Sick 11. Officers Wounded 1. Other ranks Wounded 20. 1 O.R. R.A.M.C. evacuated sick to C.C.S.	
		3 P.M.	Received orders from A.D.M.S. 40th Division to hand over Advanced Dressing Stations at PHILOSOPHE, ST. PATRICK'S and FORT GLATZ to 111th Field Ambulance on night August 8/9. Advanced parties and details of relief to be arranged between O.C. Field Ambulances concerned. Arrangements for relief made with O.C. 111th Fd. Amb. watchword "delay". An advanced party of 111th Fd.Amb. and our at PHILOSOPHE and LOOS at 9 P.M. This party divided into three and worked during	

Army Form C. 2118.

WAR DIARY
or
INTELLIGENCE SUMMARY
(Erase heading not required.)

Instructions regarding War Diaries and Intelligence Summaries are contained in F. S. Regs., Part II. and the Staff Manual respectively. Title Pages will be prepared in manuscript.

Place	Date	Hour	Summary of Events and Information	Remarks and references to Appendices
BRAQUEMONT	7		Hq moved to 137 Tr. Sub.	
	8		Received orders at 6 P.M. to send "C" Sectn 136 Tr. Sub. to HQ Tr. Sub. at LOOS filter. (LABEUVRIÈRE) on completion of relief in LOOS filter. Admission officers SWR 1 Offr. Ranks disch. 27 (Wounded 37).	
		10 a.m.	Orders issued to OC.3 Algerian Military Station at LES BREBIS and MARLE dismantling all personnel of 136 Field Ambulance at LES BREBIS to arrive & return to his proper unit back from Headquarters of 137 Tr. Sub. ?wwwwwwwwwwwwww.	
		6 p.m.	Main party of III Tr. Amb. arrived at PHILOSOPHE & took over Burial J. 137 Tr. Sub. being disch. at this place returned to BRAQUEMONT awaiting orders & P.M.	
		12 midnight	Officers NCOs and men 137 Tr. Sub. at ST. PATRICK's and FORT. GLATZ allowed by personnel of III Tr. Sub. — they returned by truck to PHILOSOPHE and headed M.	
	9	1 P.M.	Half works (BRAQUEMONT) at 1 P.M. Colonial Officers SWR 1 Other Ranks disch II Wounded 23.	
		2 P.M.	NCOs and men sent to LES BREBIS to relieve personnel of 136 F Amb. at FORT. place.	
		6 P.M.	Personnel of 136 F. Amb. returned from LES BREBIS to Headquarters (BRAQUEMONT) the whole of "C" section 136 F Amb. being now concentrated and ready to move tomorrow. M	
			Admissions O.R. DwW 5 Wounded 3	
	10	2 P.M.	"C" Sectn. 136th Field Ambulance started to LABEUVRIÈRE by march route. M	

Army Form C. 2118.

WAR DIARY
or
INTELLIGENCE SUMMARY

(Erase heading not required.)

Instructions regarding War Diaries and Intelligence Summaries are contained in F. S. Regs., Part II. and the Staff Manual respectively. Title Pages will be prepared in manuscript.

Place	Date	Hour	Summary of Events and Information	Remarks and references to Appendices
BRAQUEMONT	11		Admissions O.R. SirR 13 Wounded 4 (W)	
	12		Admissions Officers SirR 2 O.R. SirR 16 Wounded 8 (W)	
	13		Admissions Officers SirR 1 O.R. SirR 14 Wounded 7 (W)	
	14		Admissions Officers SirR 1 S.R. SirR 16 Wounded 9 (W)	
	15		1 O.R. 137th H.Arnt. evacuated to "GCS" (W) Admissions Officer SirR 1 O.R. SirR 14 Wounded 8 (W) Inspection by D.M.S. 1st Army. LIEUT. W.L. THOMAS inspected L' A.D.M.S. 16th Division for clns'. Struck off the strength of this unit.	
	16		Admissions Officers SirR 1 O.R. SirR 19 Wounded 17 4 OR's reinforcements from No 5 Base reported for duty and taken on the strength (W) Admissions Officers SirR 4 O.R. SirR 10 Wounded 8	
	17		LIEUT. C. O'MALLEY posted to Hyperites Medical Offest to 21st Bn. The Wiltshires Regiment - struck off the strength accordingly. (W) Admissions Officers SirR 1} O.R. SirR 10 Wounded 2 (W) Wounded 13	
	18		Admissions Officers Wounded 1 O.R. SirR 23 Wounded 11. 1 O.R. A.S.C. attd. H.Ornt. wounded (W)	
	19		Admissions Officers Wounded 1 O.R. SirR 25 Wounded 3 * *Details on Barrow Prisoner of to 1 O.R. A.S.C. with H.Ornt. wounded. 7th Barrow Infantry. (W)	
	20			
	21		Admissions Officers SirR 1 O.R. SirR 13 Wounded 8 (W)	

Army Form C. 2118.

WAR DIARY
or
INTELLIGENCE SUMMARY

(Erase heading not required.)

Place	Date	Hour	Summary of Events and Information	Remarks and references to Appendices
BRAQUEMONT	22		Admission O.R. Sir 16 Wounded 8 NYD	
	23		Admission O.R. Sir 14 Wounded 11.	
		11 A.M.	Received orders from A.D.M.S. 46th Division (O). to send an Advanced Dressing Station to NORTH MAROC, SOUTH MAROC and LES BREBIS. Also the Divisional Soup Kitchen and Baths at LES BREBIS. 133rd Fd. Amb. arrived and completed by 6 P.M.	
			Orders also received to take over Advanced Dressing Stations at the BREWERY PHILOSOPHE - ST. PATRICK and FORT GLATZ. Took over latter at 2 P.M. Took over place at 9 P.M.	
		30n	Hq 24th Inf. Bde. & 46th over A.D.S's at 14 B13 Section from 112th Fd. Amb. Section of 32nd Division to be attached to the Fd. Amb. to temporarily aft.	
		12 noon	H. Ambulance orders attached to the Advanced Dressing Station to report to and await further instructions.	
		1.30 p.m.	Orders received from A.D.M.S. L. to stand by and await instructions.	
		3.3 A.m.	Orders received from A.D.M.S. L. convoy to take original allotment of relief. A.D.S's attached to this effect.	
		5 p.m.	S.M.L. O.C. 111th Fd.Amb. re taking over from his unit. MAROC N. S.C. 112th Fd.Amb. re taking over 14 B20 m 24 B hrs.	
		8.30 p.m.	135th H.Amb. completed taking over as MAROC and LES BREBIS. O.C. the Advanced of this unit, previously working at MAROC and LES BREBIS proceeded to the BREWERK PHILOSOPHE direct - medical and ordnance equipment accompanied the party - reserve dressings, rations etc. as per schedule issued by D.D.M.S. 1st Army kept for recovery units.	

2449 Wt. W14957/Mg0 750,000 1/16 J.B.C. & A. Forms/C.2118/12.

Army Form C. 2118.

WAR DIARY
or
INTELLIGENCE SUMMARY

(Erase heading not required.)

Place	Date	Hour	Summary of Events and Information	Remarks and references to Appendices
BRAQUEMONT	23rd	P.M. 11.45	"B" Section 90th Fd. Amb. 32nd Division arrived to take over duty from 90th AUCHEL. Strength: 3 officers 3/4 O.R's R.A.M.C. A.S.C personnel and transport complete including 2 Motor Ambulance Cars. (1)	
	24th	A.M. 2	Reliefs at PHILOSOPHE and LOOS completed. Admissions Officers Wounded 1 O.R. Sick 15. Wounded 3 (G.35, & G.6.3) (G.35, & G.2.8)	
		8	Notified A.D.M.S. 40th Division and O.C. 90th Field Ambulance that all the Horse transport and equipment of "B" Section of this unit would be returned to AUCHEL today. They not being required. Nine Ambulance horses (any) can't remain.	
		9	"B" Section 90th Fd.Amb. 1 officer 53 O.R's proceeded by march route to BREVERY, PHILOSOPHE. 1 officer with horsed transport and 20 R's Rams proceeded by march route. ..	
			At AUCHEL. The officers in relief du on complete of reliefs. The following personnel of this section to remain at BRAQUEMONT to complete – 2 officers O.R's R.A.M.C. 4 A.S.C. M.T. 2. Arrival of 3 O.R's Rams reinforcements.	
	25/A	3 P.M.	Took over three dug-outs in 14 Bis Section from 112 Field Ambulance. O.R's 12. Dug-outs situated at G.28.d.8.3 : 5 ; G.28.d.9.3 : 4.5 ; G.29.d.8.5 . These dug-outs in the winter dails, by an officer from A.D.S, PHILOSOPHE. Admissions - Officers Sick 1 O.R. Sick 15 Wounded 1. Two Non-Comd. Officers and 6 Pvts and N.CO's British Non Sisang Stations of 111th and 113th Bd. Ambs to take over buildings and equipment pending arrival of incoming units. (1)	

WAR DIARY
or
INTELLIGENCE SUMMARY

Army Form C. 2118.

(Erase heading not required.)

Place	Date	Hour	Summary of Events and Information	Remarks and references to Appendices
BRAQUEMONT	26.		Admitted O.R's B.i.R 11 Wounded 12 AW	
	27.		Admitted Officers B.i.R 3 O.R's B.i.R 15 Wounded 1 AW	
	28.		Admitted Officers B.i.R 3 O.R's B.i.R 17 Wounded 6	
		5 P.M.	LIEUT. D. PENMAN, R.A.M.C. reported for duty and taken on the strength.	
		6 P.M.	Martin order received from A.D.M.S. 47th Division to hand over duty rids to 14 Bde Section W. a medical unit of up to 3rd Division on frontier September 1, 1916 — also to take AUCHEL L'Hym Section. AW	
			Sent day M. Section "B" Section 90th Field Ambulance AW	
	29.		Admitted Officers B.i.R 1 O.R's B.i.R 10 Wounded 7.	
		8.30 A.M.	No. 39228 Pte SIMMONDS, T. "D" Company 18th WELSH REGT. died in main dressing station from wounds.	
		12 noon	Advance Guard arrived with regard to handing over 14 BIS Section and return of "B" Section 90th Fd Amb to their unit on September 1, 1916. AW	
	30.		Admissions Officers B.i.R 3 O.R's B.i.R 22 Wounded 1	
		4.30 P.M.	No. 16177 Pte MOIRFIELD, M. 8th East Lancashire Regt died of wounds in main dressing station Admissions Officers B.i.R 3 O.R's B.i.R 11 Wounded.	
	31st.		LIEUT. C.H.C. BYRNE detailed temporarily as M.O. ic 8th Garr. Land. Rgt. 112th Bde.	
			37 Twins	
			34 N.C.O.s and men proceeded to PHILOSOPHE Advanced Dressing Station to duty.	

Signature [Lieut. Colonel, R.A.M.C. Commanding 187 Field Ambulance]

1401/734

40th Div.

131st Field Ambulance

Feb 1916

Army Form C. 2118.

Sect. F.

WAR DIARY
or
INTELLIGENCE SUMMARY.

(Erase heading not required.)

Instructions regarding War Diaries and Intelligence Summaries are contained in F. S. Regs., Part II. and the Staff Manual respectively. Title pages will be prepared in manuscript.

VOLUME IV — 137th Field Ambulance R.A.M.C.

Place	Date	Hour	Summary of Events and Information	Remarks and references to Appendices
BRAQUEMONT L25.∂.2.b.	Sept 1916 1	A.M.	Admissions Officers Sir 2 Other Ranks Sir 9 Wounded 11.	
		8.30	3 Officers 3/9 O.R's R.A.M.C. 90th Field Ambulance returned to AUCHEL L'Hygrin units. (W)	
	2		Admitted Officers Sir 3 O.R's Sir 12 Wounded 3 (W)	
	3		Admissions Officers Sir 1 O.R's Sir 4 Wounded 2.	
			1 Sergt. 137 Fd Amb evacuated sick to C.C.S.	
		11 A.M.	Received secret instructions from A.D.M.S. 46th Division to augment personnel to advanced Dressing Station, LOOS.	
		2 P.M.	on night September 3/4. 16 NCO's and men and 1 Officer despatched to A.D.S. PHILISOPHE.	
		3 P.M.	1 Officer and 16 Other Ranks similarly found from PHILOSOPHE to ST PATRICKS A.D.S. in LOOS.	
			20 extra stretchers and some number of stretchers, a good supply of wheeled stretchers and dressings etc. to 2 A.D.S's. This augmentation made in view of an expected raid. (W)	
	4		Admissions Officers Sir 2 O.R's Sir 14 Wounded 14. (W)	
			1 Sergt 137 Fd Amb evacuated sick to C.C.S.	
	5		Admissions O.R's Sir 20 Wounded 11	
			1 O.R. 137 Fd Amb. evacuated sick to C.C.S. (W)	
	6		Admissions Officers Sir 2 O.R's Sir 9 Wounded 3. (W)	
	7		Admissions Officers Sir 1 O.R's Sir 9 Wounded 12. (W)	

Army Form C. 2118.

WAR DIARY
or
INTELLIGENCE SUMMARY.
(Erase heading not required.)

Place	Date	Hour	Summary of Events and Information	Remarks and references to Appendices
BRAQUEMONT	8		Admitted Officers Sick 1 O.R's Sick 17 Wounded 14	
			1 Sergeant and 1 Pte 137 H. Coy. evacuated to C.C.S.	
			On pdg. 136 H.Cnt. joined on completion N)	
	9		Admissions O.R's Sick 10 Wounded 3' N)	
	10		Admitted O.R's Sick 6 Wounded 10 N)	
	11		Admitted Officers Sick 1 O.R's Sick 7 Wounded 11 N)	
	12		Admitted O.R's Sick 3' Wounded 3' N)	
	13		Admitted Officers Sick 1 O.R's Sick 10 Wounded 2 N)	
	14		Admitted O.R's Sick 6 Wounded 3'	
	15	11 a.m	Attached certain officer A.D.M.S. N)	
			Admissions Officers Sick 1 O.R's Sick 9 Wounded 3 N)	
			1 Medical Officer posted to duty as M.O. i/c 12 South Wales Borderers. Struck off to strength.	
	16		Admissions Officer Sick 1 O.R's Sick 13 Wounded 10.	
		4 P.M.	1 Officer 20 O.R's 136 H. Cnt. arrived fm LABEUVRIÈRE for duty.	
		1.30 P.M.	1 Officer 20 O.R's 137 H. Cnt. proceeded to LABEUVRIÈRE (1st Catg. Bad. Station) for duty.	
		8 P.M.	1 Officer 200 R's 136 H. Cnt. proceeded to Advanced Dressing Station at LOOS at PHILOSOPHE	

WAR DIARY
or
INTELLIGENCE SUMMARY.
(Erase heading not required.)

Army Form C. 2118.

Place	Date	Hour	Summary of Events and Information	Remarks and references to Appendices
BRAQUEMONT	Sept 1916 17	7AM.	20 O.R's 137 J.H.ind. arrived for duty from A.D.S's at LOOS and PHILOSOPHE	
			Admissions Officers NiR 3 O.R's NiR 10 Wounded 4	
	18		Admissions Officers NiR 1 O.R's NiR 6 Wounded 5	
		8 P.M.	12 O.R's 137 J.H.ind. proceeded to A.D.S's. LOOS and PHILOSOPHE to relieve an equal number N.W. of men who returned to Main Nuery Station. No 13369 Cpl Williams A.H. 21 Middlx shell wounds to A.S.S.	
	19		Admissions Officers NiR 1 O.R's NiR 3 Wounded 7	
			No. 21518 Pte Hanson W. 12 Suffolks died of wounds at Main Nuery Station	
			LIEUT. J.C. McGREEHIN R.A.M.C. proceeded to 3rd Division to relieve officer to stay.	
	20		Admissions O.R's NiR 4 Wounded 6	
		7.35 P.M.	Received operation order from A.D.M.S. 40th Division to Atk own Brigade in 14 Bn. Sector	
			from No. 7 Field Ambulance, 3rd Division. Relief to be completed by 8 P.M. 22nd September	
			Detail to be arranged by O.C. Units.	
		8 P.M.	1 Officer 20 O.R's returned to Nuery Station from 1st Posts Aid Stations. LABEVRRIERE	
	21		Admissions O.R's NiR 14 Wounded 8	
		10 AM	Instructions O.C. to 7 Field Ambulance and arrange for the taking over of dug-outs in 14 Bn.	
			Sector. Relief to take place during the morning of 22.	

WAR DIARY
or
INTELLIGENCE SUMMARY.
(Erase heading not required.)

Army Form C. 2118.

Instructions regarding War Diaries and Intelligence Summaries are contained in F. S. Regs., Part II. and the Staff Manual respectively. Title pages will be prepared in manuscript.

Place	Date	Hour	Summary of Events and Information	Remarks and references to Appendices
BRAQUEMONT	Sept 1916 21	AM 10.25	1 Officer 13 O.R's proceeded to PHILOSOPHE to Aug't'n Advanced Dressing Station.	N/
	22	11	Took over dug-outs in 14 Bis Section from No 7 Field Ambulance. Admission O.R's LiR 10 Wounded 3	N/
	23		LIEUT. T BLACK R.A.M.C. joined for duty from 181st Bde. R.F.A. Admission Officers LiR 2 O.R's LiR 27 Wounded 16	N/
	24		Admission Officers Sick 2 O.R's LiR 29 Wounded 11	N/
	25		Admission O.R's LiR 14 Wounded 18. 1 O.R's R.A.M.C. evacuated to C.C.S. 6 O.R's sent to A.D.S PHILOSOPHE to assist in evacuation of Battle Casualties in 14 Bis Section	N/
	26		Admission O.R's LiR 12 Wounded 17.	N/
	27		Admission O.R's LiR 17 Wounded 1.	N/
	28		Admission Officers LiR 1 O.R's LiR 14 Wounded 3	N/
	29		Admission Officers Sick 2 O.R's Sick 11 Wounded 2	N/
	30		Admission Officers Sick 2 O.R's Sick 19 Wounded 4	N/

LIEUT. H.L. McCORMICK R.A.M.C. posted as M.O. I/c 12th Batt. Welsh Borderers.

K. Mundell
LIEUT. COLONEL, R.A.M.C.
COMMANDING 187 FIELD AMBULANCE.

140/1815

40P.1000

13th Field Ambulance.

Oct 1915

COMMITTEE FOR THE
MEDICAL HISTORY OF THE WAR
Date -9 DEC. 1915

Volume V.

Army Form C. 2118.

Scene

137th Field Ambulance R.A.M.C.

WAR DIARY
or
INTELLIGENCE SUMMARY.
(Erase heading not required.)

October 1916.

Place	Date	Hour	Summary of Events and Information	Remarks and references to Appendices
BRAQUEMONT (36.B 1/40,000) L25. & 2.5.	1		Admissions O.R's SicK 13 Wounded 5'	
			1 Sergt. 137th Fd. Amb. evacuated to 1st C.C.S. (Sick)	
		12 noon	1 Officer 20 O.R's 136th Fd. Amb. arrived from LABEUVRIÈRE to duty w/ Advanced Dressing Station	
		2 P.M	Through "prisoner" from BRAQUEMONT toured w/ A.D.S. PHILOSOPHE and returned a similar number to normal w/ the same unit already at A.D.S. PHILOSOPHE. This later party returned to	
	2	3.30 P.M	BRAQUEMONT departed at 4.30 P.M. to return to LABEUVRIÈRE. N)	
			Admissions Officers Sick 1 O.R's Sick 20 Wounded 5'	
			LIEUT. D. YLIES I.D. R.A.M.C. arrived to duty from 12th South Wales Borderers – took	
			on the strength. N)	
	3		Admissions Officers Sick 3 O.R's Sick 28 Wounded 9	
		11 AM.	LIEUT. P. BLACK R.A.M.E. left to report to A.D.M.S. 3rd Division, for the strength.	
			CAPT. A.J. BEVERIDGE R.A.M.C. temporarily attached as M.O. 1/c 14th Argyll & Sutherland	
			Highlanders. 1 O.R 137th Fd. Amb. evacuated to 1st C.C.S. (Sick). N)	
	4		Admissions Officers Sick 3. Wounded 1. O.R's Sick 11 Wounded 12.	
		7 P.M.	6 R.A.M.C. reinforcements arrived from M.5th General Base Depot, taken on strength. N)	
	5		Admissions Officers Sick 1 O.R's Sick 23' Wounded 6.	

Army Form C. 2118.

Volume V

137th Field Ambulance R.A.M.C.

WAR DIARY
INTELLIGENCE SUMMARY.
(Erase heading not required.)

October 1916

Place	Date	Hour	Summary of Events and Information	Remarks and references to Appendices
BRAQUEMONT	5		A.D.S. Stationed - situated in Tritt Avenue G.29 A1, B3. Labelled evac to 19.0. & 14 D.F.A.1 (Battalion in support 1/4 Bis Leicestor) at Hyperbole Ady Post. RW	
	6		Admissions Officers Sick 2, OR's Sick 30, Wounded 12. RW	
	7		Admissions Officers Sick 2, OR's Sick 17, Wounded 9. RW	
	8	2.30 A.M	Wounded German Prisoner (165th Inf. Regt.) admitted - evacuated to No 1 C.C.S. W	
		2.30 P.M	CHOQUES.	
		3.25 A.M	Operation Order No 6 copy 5 by A.D.M.S. 46th Division received - notifying the handing over of A.D.S. SOUTH MAROC by O.C. 135th Fd Amb. to 48th Fd Amb. 37th Division at 9th Inst. RW	
			Admissions Officers Sick 4 OR's Sick 8 Wounded 24. RW	
	9		Admissions OR's Sick 19 Wounded 16	
		P.M. 1.40	1 R.A.M.C. reinforcement received No 4 General Hospital. Operation Order No 7 copy No 6 by A.D.M.S. 40th Division received stating that 137 Fd Amb. will take over the Advanced Dressing Stations in to HULLUCH Sector from 23/110 Field Ambulance 8th Division. Relief to be completed by 6 P.M. on 12th inst. Also that 137th Field Ambulance will be relieved in the LOOS, 14 BIS, HULLUCH	

Volume V   Army Form C. 2118.

Sant

WAR DIARY
INTELLIGENCE SUMMARY.
(Erase heading not required.)

137th Field Ambulance, R.A.M.C.

October 1916

Place	Date	Hour	Summary of Events and Information	Remarks and references to Appendices
BRAQUEMONT	9		Relieved by 136th Field Ambulance and will take over 1st Corps Rest Station "A" Section at LABEUVRIERE and Officers Rest Station at AIRE. Relief to be completed by 6 P.M. on 12th inst.	
	10		Admissions Officers Sick 2 O.R's Sick 17 Wounded 9 N.Y.D.	
	11		Admissions Officers Sick 2 O.R's Sick 15 Wounded 19 N.Y.D.	
		6 P.M.	Relief by 28th Fld Amb. in HULLUCH Section completed.	
LABEUVRIERE	12		Admission at BRAQUEMONT — Officers Sick 1 O.R's Sick 39 Wounded 12. Rest Station "A" Section (1st Corps) O.R's Sick 48.	
(36B.) D.17a4.3		1.30 P.M.	135th Field Ambulance evacuated Nursing Station at BRAQUEMONT and Advanced Nursing Station at LOOS, PHILOSOPHE, 14BIS and HULLUCH and handed over to 136th Field Ambulance.	
		8 P.M.	Proceeded by Motor Ambulance to LABEUVRIERE arriving at 3 P.M. Following Officers and personnel still not accompany unit :- LIEUT N. GARRARD and 20 O.R's Proceeded to AIRE on 16th and to 1st 4th Corps Officers Rest Station + LIEUT. D. PENMAN and 20 O.R's permanent to duty with 136th Field Ambulance :- 2 L.A.R's N-field 16 LE. BREBIS for duty with 2.24th Coy R.E. :- Capt. O. J. BEVERIDGE in charge of 4th Advanced Railway BETHUNE	

Volume V

Army Form C. 2118.

WAR DIARY
or
INTELLIGENCE SUMMARY.
(Erase heading not required.)

137th Field Ambulance, R.A.M.C.

October 1916

Place	Date	Hour	Summary of Events and Information	Remarks and references to Appendices
LABEUVRIERE	12		Took over 1st Posts Red: Station (A. Sector) & 1st Caps Officers Red: Station, LIRE.	
	13		Admissions O.R's Sick 32 Wounded 2	
	14		Admissions O.R's Sick 17 Wounded 1	
	15		Admissions O.R's Sick 8 Wounded 2	
	16		Admissions O.R's Sick 45 Wounded 4	
	17		Admissions O.R's Sick 9 Wounded 1	
			1 O.R. R.A.M.C. evacuated to C.C.S. sick.	
	18		Admissions O.R's Sick 46 Wounded 5	
			Plan of "Lillers" in the village drawn to scale. Billets re-numbered & labelled.	
			Two new reception rooms for in patients opened.	
			Reinforcement from Base received.	
	19		Admissions O.R's Sick 13 Wounded 12	
	20		Admissions O.R's Sick 19 Wounded 7. Sent' letter from A.D.M.S. re handing over to	
	21		Admissions O.R's Sick 26 Wounded 4	
			74th Field Ambulance arrived & made preliminary arrangements for taking over.	
			New sleeping hut for patients taken into use.	

Volume V
Secret

Army Form C. 2118.

WAR DIARY
or
INTELLIGENCE SUMMARY.   137th Field Ambulance, R.A.M.C.
(Erase heading not required.)

Place	Date	Hour	Summary of Events and Information	Remarks and references to Appendices
	October 1916			
LABEUVRIERE	22		Admissions O.R's Sick 19 Wounded 0. Heavy improvements in huildings and sanitation commenced e.g. R.A.M.C. and O.R's latrines, ablution benches, soakage pits, food safes to dining hall. W	
	23		Admissions O.R's Sick 27 Wounded 1	
		9 P.M.	R.A.M.C. Operation Order No. 8 copy No. 6 received:— The 40th Division is to be relieved by the 24th Division and withdrawn into G.H.Q. Reserve:— 137th Fd. Amb. will be relieved by 74th A Field Ambulance on 29th inst. and will march to its new area on the same date under orders of A.D.M.S. 121st Infantry Brigade:— Orders to march Field Ambulance will collect, to their from Brigade, wind intern they are working; and will arrange for the care and evacuation of the sick in their Brigade areas whilst in G.H.Q. Reserve. W	
	24	4.30 P.M.	LIEUT. J.L. SCOTT R.A.M.C. reported his arrival - posted on Strength.	
			1 Capt. R.A.M.C. transferred from No. 1 C.C.S. — 1 Pte. 137th Fd. Amb. Transferred to No. 1 C.C.S	
			Admissions O.R's Sick 10 Wounded 3 W	
	25		Admissions O.R's Sick 27 Wounded 23 W	
	26		Admissions O.R's Sick 14 Wounded 8. 1 Pte R.A.M.C. Sick L. Enfield, pending	

WAR DIARY or INTELLIGENCE SUMMARY

Army Form C. 2118.

Volume I
137th Field Ambulance, R.A.M.C.
October 1916

Place	Date	Hour	Summary of Events and Information	Remarks and references to Appendices
LABEUVRIERE	Oct 26		Discharge from H. receiving communion as Chaplain to Fd Amb.	
	27		1 O.R. A.S.C. M.T. arrived as reinforcement from 608 M.T. C. A.S.C. (taken on strength 27/10)	
			121st Inf. Bde. Operation Order No. 32 copy no. 13 received:— O.C. 137th Fd. Amb. will detail an horsed ambulance W march with each of the following — 121st Inf. Bde H.Q.	
			13th York Regt. 20th Middx. Regt. on 29th inst.	
			Admissions O.R's Sick 17. Wounded 0	
			1 Officer 20 O.R's 137th Fd. Amb. returned from 136th Fd. Amb. to which unit they had been attached.	
			20 O.R's 137th Fd. Amb. returned from 224th Fd. Cy. R.E. LES BREBIS.	
			18 O.R's " " " " 1st Corps Officers Rest-Station AIRE.	
	28		Admissions O.R's Sick 14. Wounded 4	
			1 Officer returned from 1st Corps Officers Rest-Station AIRE.	
		P.M. 3	20 O.R's and 1 Officer 74th Fd. Amb. arrived as advanced party.	
		5.30	Main body of 74th Fd. Amb. arrived at Rail Station, LABEUVRIERE.	
			2 O.R's 137th Fd. Amb. evacuated to 1 C.C.S. — sick.	
		11.45	121st Inf. Bde. Order No. 33 copy no. 13 dated 28.10.16 received — detail of march for	

Volume I

Army Form C. 2118.

WAR DIARY
or
INTELLIGENCE SUMMARY
(Erase heading not required.)

137th Field Ambulance, R.A.M.C.

October 1916

Place	Date	Hour	Summary of Events and Information	Remarks and references to Appendices
LABEUVRIERE	28		The 30th will also take 137th Fd. Amb. will detail one horsed ambulance & accompany 21st Bn Middlesex Regt. Other ambulances will march with units as already detailed.	
		8 PM	As no horsed ambulance wagon to our available – one motor ambulance wagon is being sent. Handed over 1st Coll. Post Station "A" Section to 74th Field Ambulance NJ	
	29	A.M. 7.15	Field Ambulance marched out. — 4 O.R's under Staff-Sergt and proceeded to BRUAY.	
BRUAY J 16 c 2.0. (36B 1/40,000)		9.25	Arrived at billeting area and opened up small dressing station.	
			Admissions Sick 4 (OR) B.R. Reginations (Small) fitted to all ranks in gas chamber. NJ	
	30	A.M. 9.30	Admissions O.R's Sick 1. Lieut. D. VILIESID left for BOULOGNE. Capt. J.M. LINNELL R.A.M.C. Jctn. on Tryth. Unit marched off from J16 c 2.0. and proceeded by march route via 121st Infantry Brigade to new billeting area.	
GUESTREVILLE V 13 c 1.5 (36B 1/40,000)		P.M. 3.20	Arrived in new area and opened up Dressing Station of 25 beds.	
	31	P.M. 9.40	Admissions O.R's Sick 3. 121st Bde. Preliminary Operation Order copy to 13 dated 13/10/16 received — warning unit to prepare to move to 2nd hrs L' new billeting area.	

W. M. White
LIEUT. COLONEL R.A.M.C.
COMMANDING 137 FIELD AMBULANCE

140/762

40th Div

131st Field Ambulance

COMMITTEE FOR THE
MEDICAL HISTORY OF THE WAR
Date −3 JAN. 1917

Nov. 1916

SECRET

Volume VI. November, 1916

Army Form C. 2118.

WAR DIARY
or
~~INTELLIGENCE~~ SUMMARY.

137th Field Ambulance, R.A.M.C.

(Erase heading not required.)

Place	Date	Hour	Summary of Events and Information	Remarks and references to Appendices
GUESTREVILLE 36B/40,000 V.13.c.1.5.	November 1		Unit-mobilised with base motorators. Admission Officers SiR 2 O.R's SiR 9. W	
	2	A.M. 8.15	Unit proceeded by march route to OPPY	
OPPY Renz Sheet 1/100,000		P.M. 2.15	Arrived at OPPY. Opened up small dressing station. Admissions O.R's SiR 6.	
E.3 16, 24.			2 O.R's 137th F.d. Amb. evacuated SiR to C.C.S. W	
	3	A.M. 7.30	121st F.d. Amb. Order No.36 Copy No.13 received. Orders to proceed by march route to DUTREBOIS (North of Riv. L'AUTHIE) and to be clear of OPPY by 9.30 A.M. 4th inst.	
		A.M.	3 O.R's 137th F.d. Amb. evacuated SiR to C.C.S. Admissions O.R's SiR 15. W	
	4	9.15	Left OPPY by march route and proceeded to DUTREBOIS. 121st F.d. Bde Order 37 received - unit ordered to GORGES on 5th inst.	
		P.M. 1.45	Arrived at DUTREBOIS	
DUTREBOIS Renz Sheet 1/100,000 D.4. 15.5. 10.8.			1 O.R's 137th F.d. Amb. evacuated SiR to C.C.S. Admissions O.R's SiR 16.	
		3.45	Operation Order No. 5 O.C. 121st Suffolk Regt received - this in accordance with 121st F.d. Bde. Order No 37 received this morning at 9 AM. - Unit to be South of Arrivet on Rive L'AUTHIE at 8.33 a.m. 5th inst. Route by LE QUESNAL FM. — AUTHEUX — FIENVILLERS — BERNEVIL road to GORGES.	

Army Form C. 2118.

WAR DIARY
or
INTELLIGENCE SUMMARY
(Erase heading not required.)

137th Field Ambulance, R.A.M.C.

VOLUME VI. November 1916.

Instructions regarding War Diaries and Intelligence Summaries are contained in F.S. Regs., Part II. and the Staff Manual respectively. Title pages will be prepared in manuscript.

Place	Date	Hour	Summary of Events and Information	Remarks and references to Appendices
	November			
OUTRE BOIS	5	A.M. 8.33	Unit passed starting point (bridge over Rue d'AUTHIE) and proceeded by march route to GORGES.	
GORGES		noon 12	Arrived at GORGES.	
Rem stat'l 1, 100 qtrs, C.S. 10.2.6.8.	6		Admissions. Officers Seir 1 OR's Seir 8. NJ	
			Admissions. Officers Seir 1 OR's Seir 6.	
			1 OR RAMC (137th H.Aml.) evacuated Seir. NJ	
	7		Admissions. OR's Seir 15. NJ	
	8		Admissions. OR's Seir 7.	
	9		Capt J.O.'s BEVERIDGE R.A.M.C. detached to temporary duty with No.9 C.C.S. CONTAY. NJ	
			Admissions OR's Seir 18.	
			1 OR's A.S.C. (137 H.Aml.) evacuated Seir to C.C.S. NJ	
	10		Admissions O.R's Seir 9.	
	11		2 OR's RAMC (137 H.Amb) evacuated Seir to C.C.S. NJ	
			2 OR's " " 5th Army Trench Mortar School VALHEUREUX - struck off strength.	
	11		Admissions Officers Seir 1 OR's Seir 7. NJ	
	12		Admissions. OR's Seir 5. NJ	
	13		Admissions. Officers Seir 1 OR's Seir 13. 2 reinforcements A.S.C. H.T. received	

Army Form C. 2118.

WAR DIARY
or
INTELLIGENCE SUMMARY

(Erase heading not required.)

November 1916.

Instructions regarding War Diaries and Intelligence Summaries are contained in F. S. Regs., Part II. and the Staff Manual respectively. Title pages will be prepared in manuscript.

137th Field Ambulance R.A.M.C.

Volume VI

Place	Date	Hour	Summary of Events and Information	Remarks and references to Appendices
GORGES	1916 Nov 14		Admissions. Officers Nil 3 O.R's Sick 9. NYD	
			1 O.R's R.A.M.C. evacuated to C.C.S.	
	15	A.M. 4.50	121st Infantry Brigade Order No. 39 copy to 5 received. 137th Field Ambulance to follow 12.8 B. Supply Coy. at 121st harbour from Embury - Fauny road junction at the N.E. end of BERNEUIL village at 9.40 a.m. 137th Field Ambulance proceeding to billets in MEZEROLLES, south of Farms AUTHIE.	
		9.51	Orders received from Brigade 121st Inf. Bde. amending Op. Order No 39. 137th Field Ambulance to join column at cross roads 1 mile N.E. of BERNEUIL at 10 A.M. Route for march also altered.	
MEZEROLLES		P.M. 2	Arrived. Nuns station opened.	
			2 O.R's 137th Fd. Amb. evacuated to C.C.S. (ill)	
			Admissions hil.	
	16		Admissions. Officers Nil 2 O.R's Sick 6.	
	17	A.M. 1.30	Marching Order 121st Infantry Brigade No. 40 copy No 8 received. Brigade part to march on 17th bil L'BOUQUEMAISON - LE SOUICH - BREVILLERS area. Starting Point MEZEROLLE - DOULLENS hil L'BOUQUEMAISON - LE SOUICH - BREVILLERS - HAUTE VISEE. O.C. 137th Fd. Amb. to reconnoitre ROAD at 9 A.M. - route DOULLENS - HAUTE VISEE	

Army Form C. 2118.

WAR DIARY
or
INTELLIGENCE SUMMARY.
(Erase heading not required.)

Volume VI

137th Field Ambulance R.A.M.C.

November 1916

Place	Date	Hour	Summary of Events and Information	Remarks and references to Appendices
MEZEROLLES	1916 Nov. 17		The road N.E. from HTE. VISEE, which to any one of suitable distin - South position of BOUQUEMAISON.	
"	"	A.M. 9	Reffr. MEZEROLLES. On reconnoitring road N.E. from HTE. VISEE it was found to be unsuitable for transport. So Field Ambulance proceeded by main road TOULLENS - FREVENT	
BOUQUEMAISON	"	P.M. 12.10	to BOUQUEMAISON. Arrived - opened Dressing Station. Admissions Officers Sick 1 O.R's Sick 3 1 Sergeant 137th Fd. Amb. evacuated to C.C.S.	
"	"	P.M. 8.30	121st Infantry Brigade Order No. 41 Copy No. 9 received. Brigade front to north of 18th inst. to be area SUS — ST. LEGER — WARLUZEL — HUMBERCOURT — COULLEMONT. 137th Fd. Amb. to follow 121st Bn. Suffolk Regiment. — Starting point. Level Crossing N 2 B in BOUQUEMAISON - Hour.	
"	18	A.M. 9	9 A.M. — Route Through H in LE SOUICH — Cross Roads ½ mile N of NUN F.M. — Destination S.W. portion of WARLUZEL.	
			Left BOUQUEMAISON. First starting point was altered owing to state of roads and movement of other traffic. Roads down to LENS SHEET 1/100,000 not accurate. Hard frost - roads bad.	
WARLUZEL	"	P.M. 12.30	Arrived. Opened up Dressing Station. Admissions O.R's Sick 12.	
"	19		Admission Officers Sick 1 O.R's Sick 8. 1 O.R. 137th Fd Amb. evacuated sick to C.C.S.	

WAR DIARY or INTELLIGENCE SUMMARY

Army Form C. 2118.

Volume VI.   Acheux   137th Field Ambulance R.A.M.C.
              1916

Place	Date	Hour	Summary of Events and Information	Remarks and references to Appendices
WARLUZEL	June 1916 20		Admissions. O.R's Sick 2. N.Y.	
"	21		Admission O.R's Sick 9.	
"		P.M. 9.13	121st Inf. Bde. Op. Order No. 44 Copy No. 9 received. Unit to proceed to BRETEL tomorrow. Starting point :- Cavalry cross station 1/4 mile S. of WARLUZEL. Time of passing 10.30 A.M. N.Y.	
"	22	A.M. 10	Field Ambulance marched out from WARLUZEL.	
BRETEL	"	P.M. 2.15	Unit arrived at BRETEL. Opened up Dressing Station.	
"	"	9	121st Inf. Bde. Op. Order No. 45 Copy No. 10 received. Unit to be clear of BRETEL at 8.15 A.M. 23rd inst. Route :- GEZAINCOURT — X in BAGNEUX — LONGUEVILLETTE — FIENVILLERS — BERNEUIL — cross roads at last 'S' in F.M. du BOIS des DAMES — PERNOIS. Billets to be notified later.	
"	"		Admissions. O.R's Sick 11. N.Y.	
"	23	A.M. 3	Instructions received from Hd. Qrs. 121 Inf. Bde. that Ambulance Unit would be in PERNOIS.	
"	"	8	Fd. Ambulance left for PERNOIS. March delayed by 18th Bn. Welch Regt. crossing roads from outside BRETEL, also some of the roads were unfavorable to transport and unit had to be changed.	
PERNOIS	"	P.M. 2.25	Arrived at PERNOIS — opened up Dressing Station. Admissions. O.R's Sick 3.	

Army Form C. 2118.

WAR DIARY
or
INTELLIGENCE SUMMARY.
(Erase heading not required.)

137th Field Ambulance R.A.M.C

Volume VI

Instructions regarding War Diaries and Intelligence Summaries are contained in F.S. Regs., Part II. and the Staff Manual respectively. Title pages will be prepared in manuscript.

November 1916

Place	Date	Hour	Summary of Events and Information	Remarks and references to Appendices
PERNOIS	1916 Nov. 23	P.M. 6.50	121st. Inf. Bde. Operation Order No. 46 copy No. 9 received. Unit to leave road junction ½ mile W of BERTEAUCOURT CHURCH at 9.43 a.m. tomorrow. Route ST. LEGER - lès - DOMART - STA - L'ETOILE - road along N bank of R. SOMME. Billets PONT REMY.	
		10.10	121st. Inf. Bde. Operation Order No. 46 (after order) received. Owing to state of roads the route for time of starting Battalion changed - route for Field Ambulance as above. W	
	24	A.M. P.M. 4.30	Unit arrived at PONT REMY. Roads in a bad condition. Head of Unit reached Detraining. O.R's Sick 3	
PONT REMY	25	P.M. 3.40	121st. Inf. Bde. Operation Order No. 47 copy No. 9 received. Unit to leave for L'ETOILE tomorrow. Starting point - the road junction at FRANCIERES at 2.M in SOMME R⁴. Time of leaving starting point 10 A.M. Notification received from A.D.M.S. 40th Division passed under the administration of the 4th Army, XV Corps, on and from the 24th inst. All ordinary sick are being evacuated to AMIENS. Admissions Officers Sick 1 O.R's Sick 13. W	
	26	A.M. 9.30	Unit left for L'ETOILE.	

WAR DIARY
or
INTELLIGENCE SUMMARY

137th Field Ambulance R.A.M.C.

November 1916.

Place	Date	Hour	Summary of Events and Information	Remarks and references to Appendices
L'ETOILE	Nov. 26	P.M. 12.20	Unit arrived. Opened up Dressing Station. Admissions O.R's SeIR 2 W	
"	27		Admissions O.R's SeIR 13 W	
"	28		Admissions O.R's SeIR 10 W	
"	29		Admissions O.R's SeIR 3. Found Dressing Station t' more commodious premises — accomodation for 66 cases. W	
"	30		Admissions O.R's SeIR 3. Cases now t' be evacuated t' No 2 Stationary Hospital.	
ABBEVILLE.				

N. McIntosh
LIEUT. COLONEL, R.A.M.C.
COMMANDING 137 FIELD AMBULANCE.

140/903

40th Div.

N.º 1 Field Ambulance

Dec. 1916

COMMITTEE FOR THE
MEDICAL HISTORY OF THE WAR
Date   31 JAN. 1917

SECRET

Instructions regarding War Diaries and Intelligence Summaries are contained in F.S. Regs., Part II. and the Staff Manual respectively. Title pages will be prepared in manuscript.

Army Form C. 2118.

WAR DIARY
or
INTELLIGENCE SUMMARY
(Erase heading not required.)

Volume No. VII

Vol 7 137th Field Ambulance R.A.M.C.

December 1916

Place	Date	Hour	Summary of Events and Information	Remarks and references to Appendices
L'ETOILE (Cans. sheet 10.II 1/100,000)	Dec 1916 1		Admission Sick O.R's 12 M/J	
	2		Admissions Officer Sick 1 O.R's Sick 8 M/J	
	3		Admissions O.R's Sick 9 M/J	
	4		Admissions O.R's Sick 10 M/J	
	5		Admission O.R's Sick 15 M/J	
	6		Admissions O.R's Sick 11	
			1 O.R. 137th 91 Coy. R.E. sent to 1 O.R. C.I.C. attd 137 "D.Unit evacuated sick to" C.C.S. M/J	
	7	P.M. 12.40	Reports from no. 1 more & Stores received – stating particulars as to Ration Transport and "Sanitary" – Sent direct from Hd.Qrs. 46th Division.	
		8.10	121st Inf. Bde. No 333 (9) received – stating Particulars as to advance and billetting parties to proceed area of the Brigade front.	
			1 O.R's A.S.C. attd 137th Field Ambulance evacuated sick to "C.C.S"	
	8		Admissions Officers Sick 1 O.R's Sick 16 M/J	
		P.M. 12.25	121st Inf. Bde. Operation Order 48 copy no. 7 received – stating detail of Personnel & accompany transport by road and arrangements for conveyance of rest of Personnel by rail. The 137th Inf. Bde. Corps to move into XV Corps Middle Area to see 10th and 11th Personnel entraining at "LONGPRE-LES-CORPS-SAINTS"	

T2134. Wt. W708-776. 500000. 4/15. Sir J.C.&S.

SECRET

Army Form C. 2118.

WAR DIARY
or
INTELLIGENCE SUMMARY
(Erase heading not required.)

December 1916. 137th Field Ambulance R.A.M.C.

Volume No. VII

Place	Date	Hour	Summary of Events and Information	Remarks and references to Appendices
L'ETOILE	Dec 8th		detachment at 'DERNANCOURT'. Transpt. to proceed by road and Rail to 'A' Coy offices of F.A. 137/11"	
		P.M. 1.35'	Sec. N.' ST SAUVEUR instructions of Brig. Genl. (Capt. Littlewood R.A.M.C.) who had Coy No. 12.	
			40th Division R.A.M.C. wire to A.13 Cpy A3 received = stating that Fd. Amb. would move from forward	
			area under orders of D.D.M.S. 121st Inf. Bde.	
	9		Admissions Officers Sick 1 O.Rs Sick 13 M	
	10	A.M. 8.30	Admissions Officers Sick 1 O.Rs Sick 20 M	
		9.21	Admissions O.Rs Sick 12. Transpt. of unit. Capt. P.M.EDWARDS R.A.M.C. proceeded to ST SAUVEUR	
			121st Inf. Bde. Hd. to 'A' Coy by 7 received = Arrival of unit. to proceed by road from LINGRE =	
		10.30 A.M. 11 hrs.	LES-CORPS-SAINTS at 10.30 A.M. 11 hrs. to 'EDGEHILL' (DERNANCOURT) from destroying Stn.	
			Unit to proceed by road route to 'EDGEHILL' in SAILLY-LAURETTE.	
			CAPT. A.J.BEVERIDGE R.A.M.C. rcvd. 1 Fd. Amb. to A.D. Army School of Musketry POINT REMY to duty Strk. attached	
			on Fd. Amblces. Car and one truck M.T. detailed to same School on temporary duty.	
			1 O.R's 137" M.Amb. evacuated sick to C.C.S. M	
	11	A.M. 9.10	Admissions 3 O.Rs 137 Fd. Amb. evacuated sick to C.C.S.	
	"	9.10	Unit marched out to entrainment at LONGPRE	
		12 noon	Unit entrained.	

SECRET

Army Form C. 2118.

WAR DIARY
or
INTELLIGENCE SUMMARY

(Erase heading not required.)

137th Field Ambulance R.A.M.C.

December 1916

Volume VII

Place	Date	Hour	Summary of Events and Information	Remarks and references to Appendices
SAILLY-LAURETTE	Dec 11	7.15 PM	Unit arrived after 3 hours march from detraining station (EDGEHILL). Roads and weather very bad. Unable to open up Dressing Station owing to lack of accommodation. A.J.	
"	12		Admissions O.R's Sick 1. Opened up Dressing Station – accommodation 20 patients. A.J.	
"	13		Admissions Officers Sick 1. O.R's Sick 13. A.J.	
"	14		Admissions Officers Sick 1. O.R's Sick 15. A.J.	
"	15	3.10 PM	Admission O.R's Sick 7. 121st Inf. Bde. order to S.O. received – detailing certain movement of the Battalions of the Brigade. A.J.	
"	16		Admissions O.R's Sick 5. A.J.	
"	17		Admissions O.R's Sick 2. A.J. Lieut. J.L. SCOTT, R.A.M.C. posted as M.O. 1/c 19th Bn. Royal Welsh Fusiliers, Short of History A.J.	
"	18		Admissions Officers Sick 1. O.R's Sick 2. Capt. A.J. BEVERIDGE, R.A.M.C. reported from 4th Army School of Anaesthetics, PONT REMY. – Taken on strength. A.J.	
"	19		Admissions O.R's Sick 14. Capt. A.J. BEVERIDGE, R.A.M.C. detailed for duty with 1st Bn. XV Corps. Capt. A.R. POLLOCK, R.A.M.C. taken on strength – attached to duty 21/4 Army School of Anaesthetics. Lieut. N. GARRARD and Lieut. D. PENMAN, R.A.M.C. detailed for duty, temporarily, XV Corps Rest Station. A.J.	
"	20	8.4 PM	Admissions O.R's Sick 7. 121st Inf. Bde. S.P. Order No. 51, 6th Dec. 7 received, stating that 40th Division would relieve 33rd Division in the Rifle section of the Corps Front. 121 Inf. Bde. to relieve Sumner Kleber on December 27.	

SECRET

Army Form C. 2118.

Instructions regarding War Diaries and Intelligence
Summaries are contained in F.S. Regs., Part II.
and the Staff Manual respectively. Title pages
will be prepared in manuscript.

WAR DIARY
or
INTELLIGENCE SUMMARY.
(Erase heading not required.)

December 1916
Volume VII.

137th Field Ambulance R.A.M.C.

Place	Date	Hour	Summary of Events and Information	Remarks and references to Appendices
SAILLY-LAURETTE	21		Admission O.R's Sick 3 NJ	
	22		Admission O.R's Sick 7	
		P.M. 12.40	Order received from A.D.M.S. 40th Division to send Two tent subdivisions (one officer) for duty at XV Corps Rest Station Camp 12b.	
		3.15	Two tent subdivisions (one officer and 30 other ranks) with the exception of 1 W.O., 1 cpl and 1 n.c.e, proceeded to XV Corps Rest Station. NJ	
			Admission O.R's Sick 4	
	23	P.M. 4.33	40th Division R.A.M.C. Order No 14 copy No 6 received — stating that 137th Field Ambulance less two tent subdivisions will move to Camp 17 on the 27th inst. and make arrangements for the reception of the rest of the Manne Brigade. Field Ambulance to move independent of Brigade. NJ	
			Admissions O.R's Sick 7	
	24	A.M. 9	2/Lt 137 Field Amb. proceeded to personally liaise with Lee and 32 Brigadier R.E.C. O.C. unit with QM and Sergeant Major proceeded to Camp 17 to interview O.C. 19th Field Ambulance, 33rd Division, and made arrangements for leading in advance party to little Camp on 26th inst. Details for taking over accommodation arranged. NJ	
	26	A.M. 8.45	Trench Table in connection with 121st Brigade Order No 311 of 20-12-16 received	

SECRET

Army Form C. 2118.

Instructions regarding War Diaries and Intelligence Summaries are contained in F.S. Regs., Part II. and the Staff Manual respectively. Title pages will be prepared in manuscript.

WAR DIARY
or
INTELLIGENCE SUMMARY.
(Erase heading not required.)

137th Field Ambulance R.A.M.C.
Volume VII
December 1916

Place	Date	Hour	Summary of Events and Information	Remarks and references to Appendices
SAILLY-LAURETTE	25th		137th Fd Amb. LN. north bank ailes of LL 21 Camp 17 on 27th Nil — Nil. 21 bank on L'.	
			BRAY - CORBIE Road before 11.45 a.m.	
	26		Admissions Officers SickR 1. O.R's SickR 8	
			Admissions Officers SickR 2. O.R's SickR 23 Nil	
			6 O.R's 137th Fd Amb evacuated SickR to C.C.S. Nil	
	27		Admissions Officers SickR 1. O.R's SickR 38 Wounded 1	
		A.M. 11	Unit (less SAILLY LAURETTE and proceeded by march route to Camp 17 SUZANNE. Nil	
SUZANNE		P.M. 3.30	Unit (less 2 Tent Subdivision personnel) arrived TOR and Dressing Station recently vacated by 101st Fd Amb.	
	28		Admissions Officers SickR 1. O.R's SickR 10 Wounded 1	
			Opened up dressing station in Camp 21 SUZANNE - accommodation 5 Officers, 75 patients. Nil	
			In Dressing Station Camp 17, extended to 75 patients. Nil	
	29		Admissions O.R's SickR 40 Nil	
	30		Admissions O.R's SickR 32 Nil	
	31	A.M. 9	Admissions O.R's SickR 18	
			CAPTAIN P.W. EDWARDS, R.A.M.C. proceeded to 2/1st Wilks Yeo Ft Tipton 148th Bde M.O.	

R. Wyndale
LIEUT. COLONEL
R.A.M.C.
COMMANDING 1ST FIELD AMBULANCE

T2134. Wt. W708—776. 500000. 4/15. Sir J. C. & S.

134th Field Ambulance

COMMITTEE FOR THE
MEDICAL HISTORY OF THE WAR
Date 13 MAR. 1917

SECRET

Army Form C. 2118.

WAR DIARY
INTELLIGENCE SUMMARY.
(Erase heading not required.)

137th Field Ambulance. R.A.M.C.

VOLUME VIII.   Vol 8

January 1917

Place	Date	Hour	Summary of Events and Information	Remarks and references to Appendices
	January			
CAMP 17	1		Admission Officers Sick 1. O.R's Sick 47. NJ	
near SUZANNE	2		Admissions. Officers Sick 2. O.R's Sick 41. NJ	
(Wood huts)	3		Admissions. O.R's Sick 56. NJ 28 O.R's R.A.M.C. arrived from No 1 Territorial Base Dépôt as reinforcements	
G 8 b 5.7.	4		Admissions. O.R's Sick 57. Wounded 1. 1 NCO 137th 2/Lond evacuated to C.C.S. NYD	
	5		Capt. P.W. Edwards R.A.M.C. returned from 21st Middlesex NYK. NJ	
	5		Admissions Officers Sick 1 O.R's Sick 26. NJ	
	6		Admissions Officers Sick 2. O.R's Sick 33. NJ	
	7		Admissions Officers Sick 5/ Wounded 1. O.R's Sick 38 Wounded 1. NJ	
	8		Admissions O.R's Sick 40 Wounded 1. Captain J.W. Linnell, R.A.M.C. attached as M.O. 1/c 19th Captain A.J. Beveridge R.A.M.C. returned from temporary duty". NJ	
			Royal Welsh Fusiliers (temporary duty.)	
			XVth Corps LAUNDRY	
	9		Admission Officers Sick 4 O.R's Sick 32 Wounded 1.	
			Captain J.O'S. Beveridge, R.A.M.C. evacuated Sick to CCS - struck off strength	
			1 O.R's R.A.M.C. evacuated sick to CCS - struck off strength. NJ	
	10		Admissions. Officers Sick 1. O.R's Sick 34. Capt A.J. Beveridge R.A.M.C. detached for duty as	
			M.O. 1/c 40th Div. Ard. Major Fried. NJ	

SECRET

Army Form C. 2118.

Instructions regarding War Diaries and Intelligence
Summaries are contained in F. S. Regs., Part II.
and the Staff Manual respectively. Title pages
will be prepared in manuscript.

WAR DIARY
of
INTELLIGENCE SUMMARY.

(Erase heading not required.)

137th Field Ambulance R.A.M.C.

January 1917.

VOLUME VIII.

Place	Date	Hour	Summary of Events and Information	Remarks and references to Appendices
CAMP 17.	JAN. 11		Admissions officers Nil 2 O.R's Sick 36. 3 O.R's R.A.M.C. mi-infermes received from No.1 T.F. Base Depot. Taken on strength. Nil	
	12		Admissions officers Nil 2 O.R's Sick 40 Wounded 1. 2 O.R's R.A.M.C. evacuated – on tour to C.C.S. – on to U.K. for Munition Work. Nil	
	13		Capt. J.W. Linnell R.A.M.C. reported to duty from 19th Royal Welsh Fusiliers. Nil Admissions officers Nil 3 O.R's Sick 42. Nil	
	14		Admissions O.R's Sick 36. Nil	
	15		Capt. A.J. Beveridge, R.A.M.C. returned from duty with 40th Div. Ant. Argyll & Sutherland Highlanders. Proceeded to temporary duty with 14th Argyll and Sutherland Highlanders. Admissions O.R's Sick 43. 1 O.R's R.A.M.C. evacuated Sick to C.C.S. Nil	
	16		Admissions officers Sick 1 O.R's Sick 39. Capt. A.J. Beveridge R.A.M.C. returned from temporary duty with 14th A.& S.H. and proceeded to temporary duty as "A" Coy XV Fd. Amb. Captain J.W. Linnell, R.A.M.C. proceeded to temporary duty with 14th A.& S.H. 1 O.R's R.A.M.C. evacuated Sick to C.C.S. – 1 O.R's R.A.M.C. sent to U.K. for Munition Work. Nil	
	17		Admissions officers Sick 2 O.R's Sick 38. Nil	
	18		Admissions officers Sick 2 O.R's Sick 39. Capt. J.W. Linnell returned from duty with 14th A.T.S.H. Nil	

Army Form C. 2118.

SECRET.
Instructions regarding War Diaries and Intelligence Summaries are contained in F.S. Regs., Part II. and the Staff Manual respectively. Title pages will be prepared in manuscript.

WAR DIARY
or
INTELLIGENCE SUMMARY

137th Field Ambulance, R.A.M.C.
January 1917
Volume 8.

(Erase heading not required.)

Place	Date	Hour	Summary of Events and Information	Remarks and references to Appendices
Camp 17	JAN 19		Admissions. Officers Sick 1. O.R's Sick 43. Wounded 1. Took over Batty in Camp 21. All	
	20		Admissions. Officers Sick 1. O.R's Sick 45.	Nil
		AM 11.45	40th Division R.A.M.C. Operation Order 15 Copy 49.10 received. Stating :- The 8th Division is to relieve the 40th Division in BOUCHAVESNES NORTH SECTOR on 26/27 JAN, and in RANCOURT Sector on night 27/28 JAN. The 137th Field Ambulance will hand over detention huts in Camp 17 and 21 and Batty in Camp 21 to relieving parties of 26th Field Ambulance on 28th inst.	
	21		Admissions Officers Sick 2. O.R's Sick 49.	Nil
			During this period an average of 250 nursing sick are seen by the Field Amb. in Camps 17 and 21.	Nil
	22		Admissions. O.R's Sick 74.	
	23		Admissions. Officers Sick 4. O.R's Sick 62. 1 O.R's A.S.C. Attd. 137th Ft. Amb. evacuated thro' to C.C.S.	Nil
		PM 8	121st Inf. Bde. Op. Order No 519 Copy No 7 received. Stating :- Division is to be relieved by 3rd Bgde. 121st Inf. Bde. will be relieved by 24th Inf. Bde. on 25th January and move by march route to "L" Camps 12 and 13. Billeting party of 137th Ft. Amb. to report to Area Commandant, CHIPILLY. Starting Point, Church SUZANNE - time to form 11.43 AM - route SUZANNE - BRAY - Destination CHIPILLY.	Nil

SECRET.

Instructions regarding War Diaries and Intelligence Summaries are contained in F. S. Regs., Part II. and the Staff Manual respectively. Title pages will be prepared in manuscript.

Army Form C. 2118.

WAR DIARY
or
INTELLIGENCE SUMMARY
(Erase heading not required.)

January 1917   Volume VIII   137th Field Ambulance R.A.M.C.

Place	Date	Hour	Summary of Events and Information	Remarks and references to Appendices
CAMP 17	JAN 24		Admission Officers Sick 1. O.R's Sick 44. LIEUT. J. DUNDON, R.A.M.C. reported for duty from BASE - taken on strength 4 O.R's R.A.M.C. arrived from Base at Montrecourt.	
		PM 3.15	Amended to 131st Inf. Bde. Order No 8/9 received - 137th Fd. Amb. to proceed to Camp 12 instead of CHIPILLY and to lift over accommodation from 26th Fd. Amb. - Advance parties to arrive at Camp 12 by 8 a.m. 25/10 inst.	
	25		Admissions O.R's Sick 2. Balance party proceeded to Camp 12 at 6.30 A.M.	
		noon 12	Unit left SUZANNE (Camp 17) and proceeded by road and to Camp 12 (CHIPILLY).	
		PM 4	Unit arrived at Camp 12 - opened up Divisional station.	
	26		Admissions Officers Sick 1 O.R's Sick 2.	
	27		Admissions Officers Sick 2 O.R's Sick 14.	
	28		Admissions Officers Sick - O.R's Sick 4	
	29		Admissions Officers Sick 2 O.R's Sick 28	
		PM 6.30	R.A.M.C. Operation Order No 16 Copy No 3 received - stating that 40th Station is to be H.Q. Reserve from 26th inst. inclusive and is to be ready to entrain at 47 hours notice after receipt of Order.	
	30		Admissions Officers Sick 1 O.R's Sick 15	
	31		Admissions Officers Sick - O.R's Sick 20	

Manville Capt. R.A.M.C.
Commanding 137 Field Ambulance

140/1991

40 R. Res.

137th Field Ambulance.

Feb. 1917
S

COMMITTEE FOR THE
MEDICAL HISTORY OF THE WAR
Date 4 - APR. 1917

WAR DIARY
INTELLIGENCE SUMMARY

Army Form C. 2118.

137th Field Ambulance R.A.M.C.

February 1917 Volume IX

Place	Date	Hour	Summary of Events and Information	Remarks and references to Appendices
Camp 12 (CHIPILLY)	Oct 1		Admitting Officers Sick 3, O.R's 16 Sick, 1 O.R. A.S.C. attached 137th Fd Amb Evacuated Sick to C.C.S. M.	
	2	PM 2.55	Admitting Officers Sick 1, O.R's Sick 22 Continuation of R.A.M.C. Operation Orders No 16 Copy No 3 issued unit CM Slight evacuation marches & portable marches & Entraining station M Admissions Sick E.C.C.S. M	
	3		Admissions O.R's Sick 13. 2 O.R's R.A.M.C. evacuated Sick E.C.C.S. M.	
	4		Admissions Officers Sick 1, O.R's Sick 13 M	
	5		Admissions Officers Sick 2, O.R's Sick 10. 3 O.R's R.A.M.C. Evacuated G 79th Heavy Artillery Group M	
	6		Admissions O.R's Sick 17. 1 O.R. R.A.M.C. returned from Base as reinforcement M	
	7	PM 2:0	Admissions O.R's Sick 9. 1 O.R R.A.M.C. evacuated Sick to C.C.S. Continuation of 40th Division R.A.M.C. Operation Order No 16 Copy No 3 Received orders further details as to March Routes to & Entraining duty with XV Corps Many Rgm Rgms at Agny. Lieut F. DUNDON detailed for this duty with XV Corps Many Rgm M	
	8	PM 2.20	Admissions Officers Sick 2, O.R's Sick 24. 1 O.R R.A.M.C. + 1 O.R. A.S.C. attached 137 Fd Amb evacuated to C.C.S. 40th Division R.A.M.C. Operation Order No 17 Copy No 11 issued - 35th & 1st & 40th Division to be known as 6th & 8th Division in XV Corps Sector & the 11th & 12th Divisions will become the 5th Army Division of the XV Corps M	

SECRET

Army Form C. 2118.

Instructions regarding War Diaries and Intelligence Summaries are contained in F.S. Regs., Part II. and the Staff Manual respectively. Title Pages will be prepared in manuscript.

WAR DIARY
or
INTELLIGENCE SUMMARY

(Erase heading not required.)

137th Field Ambulance, R.A.M.C.

Sept 1917 No. 9

Place	Date	Hour	Summary of Events and Information	Remarks and references to Appendices
Camp 12 (CHIPILLY)	Sept 8	P.M. 2.20	137th Fld Amb will march from Camp 12 to billets at Bray on the 10th inst. and will take over PRIEZ FARM, MAUREPAS and Brown posts after RANCOURT Section from 2/5th Fd Amb on 15th. Staff will take over Advanced Dressing Station at PINNEY'S POST, LE FOREST and CRAMIÈRES from 5th Div. on 15th Same date. J.M.	
	9	A.M. 9.40	Ambulance Officers seen 3 O.R's Ber.15. 10.R. RAMC reported sick, 111th Bgde Group with 119th Bgde Orders Nos 63 Capt. No ID received. Seven O.R's Bgde to Rest Stn. march into Camp 12 + 21 + Lt. Bray according to detail, L/Cpl. & Pte. billeted at Fd Amb'Hd Qrs 137 Fd Amb. All Cooking and duties in the line to billets in Bray J.M.	
	10		Ambulance Officers seen 1. O.R's Ber 28. Under orders Camp 12 3.30 p.m. and proceeded by march route to billets in BRAY arriving 6.30 p.m. Advanced Parties left Camp 12 to take over mentioned Advance Dressing Stns. at 9 a.m. J.M.	
BRAY (Albert Sheet 40,000 L.15.d.5.7)	11	P.M. 1.30	Ambulance Officers seen 1. O.R's Ber 23. Main parties for Advanced Dressing Stations leave BRAY at 2.50 a.m. J.M. Relief completed in full.	
	13		2 O.R's RAMC admitted as sick + wounded.	
	14	A.P.L. 11	A.D.M.S. intimates received stating that any sick or wounded of 1st Division arriving at PINNEY'S POST are to be evacuated to "XV Corps" Main Dressing Station by the unit. J.M.	
			CAPT. J.W. LINNELL, R.A.M.C. attached for duty at Advanced Dressing Post, PINNEY'S POST. M.J. 11.02.59 137th Fd Amb. attd 2/Lieut A.R. Cadlett 1st MAUREPAS for duty with 229 Bty. R.E.	

Wt. W14957/M90 730,000 1/16 J.B.C. & A. Forms/C.2118/12.

SECRET.

Army Form C. 2118.

WAR DIARY
or
INTELLIGENCE SUMMARY
(Erase heading not required.)

Instructions regarding War Diaries and Intelligence Summaries are contained in F.S. Regs., Part II. and the Staff Manual respectively. Title Pages will be prepared in manuscript.

February 1917   Volume 9.   137th Field Ambulance, R.A.M.C.

Place	Date	Hour	Summary of Events and Information	Remarks and references to Appendices
BRAY	15		19 O.R's 137th Fd.Amb. detached as working party with 229th, 231st, R.E.	
	17	P.M. 1.30	13 O.R's 137th Fd.Amb. detached for duty with 14.5 C.C.S.	
			14 O.R's 137th Fd.Amb. detached for duty with No. 48 C.C.S.	
			3 O.R's arrived as reinforcements from Base Depôt Rouen - taken on the strength.	
	19		Lieut. N. GARRARD, R.A.M.C. transferred to U.K. and struck off strength.	
			Capt. F.B. McCARTER 136th Fd.Amb. attchd. 137th Fd.Amb. posted to 4.17 H.L.I. as R.M.O.	
			Lieut. D.A.H. MOSES 136th Fd.Amb. attchd. for duty - attchd. ADS. LEPRIEZ F.M.	
		P.M. 1	Capt. P.W. EDWARDS, R.A.M.C. assumed command of A.D.S. LE PRIEZ F.M. Instructions received from A.D.M.S. 48th Division to hand over to Advanced Bearer Posts at LE GRANIER and LE FOREST to 28th Fd.Amb. 8th Division on the 21st inst.	
	20		14 O.R's R.A.M.C. returned from duty at 48 C.C.S.	
			10 O.R's R.A.M.C. proceeded to A.B.P. MAUREPAS for duty, as working party, at R.N.S. LE PRIEZ F.M.	
	21		1 O.R. 137th Fd.Amb. evacuated sick to C.C.S. N.Y.D. Handed over A.B.P's LE FOREST and LE GRANIER	
	22		10 O.R's 137th Fd.Amb. evacuated sick to C.C.S. N.Y.D. to 25th Fd.Amb. 8th Division N.Y.D.	
	24		1 O.R. A.S.C. M.T. attchd. 137th Fd.Amb. evacuated sick to C.C.S. N.Y.D.	
	25		Lieut. D. PENMAN R.A.M.C. transferred to 33rd Division. N.Y.D.	
	26		1 O.R. 137th Fd.Amb. evacuated sick to C.C.S. N.Y.D.	
	27	P.M. 1	Lieut. J. DUNDON R.A.M.C. returned for duty from 15th Corps Main Dressing Station. N.Y.D.	
	28	5	Instructions received from A.D.M.S. 40th Division to have the unit ready to move at 3 hours notice. Intimation received from A.D.M.S. 40th Division to hand in as much of salvage & clothing of stores to Salvage Dump.	

W. Murdoch
LIEUT. COLONEL.
COMMANDING 137 FIELD AMBULANCE.

140/2086

137th F.A.

COMMITTEE FOR THE
MEDICAL HISTORY OF THE WAR
Date 6 JUN. 1917

Army Form C. 2118.

WAR DIARY
or
INTELLIGENCE SUMMARY
(Erase heading not required.)

137th Field Ambulance

March, 1917

Volume X

Place	Date	Hour	Summary of Events and Information	Remarks and references to Appendices
	March			WO 10
BRAY L.15.d.5.9. (Albert Sheet 1/40,000)	1		2 O.R's 137th Fd. Amb. evacuated sick to C.C.S.	
	3	9 A.M.	One horsed-ambulance wagon, two large motor ambulance cars and three Soyer's stoves went to Pioneer Beach Poste. MAUREPAS for distribution as follows:- one horsed ambulance wagon and one car to MAUREPAS, two cars and one Soyer's stove to A.D.S. PRIEZ FM, and one Soyer's stove to A.R.P. PINNEYS POST. Remained at A.D.S. and A.R.P. received at tiffin :- 6 extra bearers to Regimental Aid Posts Left Bn:. 1 M.O. and 4 pts. to A.R.P. MOONEYS, ten pvivate to A.D.S. PRIEZ FM and 26 pvivate to Reserve R.P. MAUREPAS. This in view of an offensive to be undertaken by the 8th Division on our	
		P.M. 4.40	R.A.M.C. Order (40th Division) No. 18 Copy No 11 received - stating that the 40th Division is to hand over the RANCOURT Section to 8th Division and will take over the front now held by the 33rd Division during period 6th - 9th inst. 137th Fd. Amb. will relieve 99th Fd. Amb. and take over existing Bearer Posts and Advanced Dressing Station on being relieved by a Fd. Amb. of the 8th Division.	
	5th	A.M. 11	Orders received from A.D.M.S. 40th Division to hand over A.D.S. PRIEZ FM. and A.R.P's in RANCOURT Section to 25th Fd. Amb. 8th Division. To hand over A.R.P. PINNEYS POST to 24th Fd. and 8th Division. To take over A.R.P's in CLERY Section from 99th relief to be completed by midnight 7/8 March.	

SECRET

Army Form C. 2118.

Instructions regarding War Diaries and Intelligence Summaries are contained in F.S. Regs., Part II. and the Staff Manual respectively. Title pages will be prepared in manuscript.

WAR DIARY
or
INTELLIGENCE SUMMARY.
(Erase heading not required.)

137th Field Ambulance, R.A.M.C.

March 1917 Volume X

Place	Date	Hour	Summary of Events and Information	Remarks and references to Appendices
BRAY	March 5		Fd. Amb. and A.D.S. HEM from same unit - reliefs in A.B.P's to be completed by midnight 8/9 March - main parts "L" stato ora A.D.S. HEM on 9th March.	
	6	P.M. 5.H.S.	1 O.R. R.A.M.C. evacuated sick to C.C.S.	
			26 O.R's 137th Field Ambulance returned to HdQrs from R.B. working parts, MAUREPAS	
			1 O.R. R.A.M.C. evacuated sick to C.C.S.	
	7	P.M. 4	A.B.P. PINNEYS POST handed over to 24th Field Ambulance 8th Division	
		5	Advanced parties of 137th Fd. Amb. arrived at A.D.S. HEM from A.D.S. PRIEZ FM. and A.B.P.s PINNEYS POST and MAUREPAS - parts under command of CAPT. J.W. LINNELL, RAMC and LIEUT. J. DUNDIN RAMC	
	7/8 Midnight		A.B.P. MURNEYS and A.D.S. PRIEZ FM. - A.B.P. MAUREPAS and all Field Ambulance arrangements in the RANCOURT SECTOR handed over to 4" 25th Field Ambulance 8th Division N.J. A.D.S. HEM	
	8	12	CAPT. P.N. EDWARDS, RAMC and rear party from PRIEZ FM. and MAUREPAS arrived at A.D.S. HEM	
			42 O.R's 137th Fd. Amb. arrived at A.D.S. HEM from Fd. Amb. HdQrs. BRAY	
		2	30 O.R's 136th Fd. Amb. (attached 137th Fd. Amb.) arrived at R.A.P's - A.B.P's and the A.D.S. HEM from 1st Fd. Amb. H.Q.s SUZANNE During afternoon and evening mob at R.A.P's - A.B.P's - and the A.D.S. HEM were taken over and	
	8/9 Midnight		99th Fd. Amb. 33rd Division. Relief of 99" Fd. Amb. by Right Sec'n "XV" Corps Trench Complete	

SECRET

Army Form C. 2118.

WAR DIARY
or
INTELLIGENCE SUMMARY.
(Erase heading not required.)

March 1917 Volume X 137th Field Ambulance R.A.M.C.

Instructions regarding War Diaries and Intelligence Summaries are contained in F.S. Regs., Part II. and the Staff Manual respectively. Title pages will be prepared in manuscript.

Place	Date	Hour	Summary of Events and Information	Remarks and references to Appendices
HEM (Albert Sheet 1/40,000 H 8 a.2.7.)	9	P.M. 1	Headquarters of 137th Fd.Amb. arrived at A.D.S. HEM from BRAY.	
	10		1 O.R. R.A.M.C. evacuated sick to C.C.S.	
	12		CAPT. C.J. YOUNG. R.A.M.C. and LIEUT. R.D. MACGREGOR R.A.M.C. arrived for duty & taken on the strength.	
			9 O.R's R.A.M.C. arrived as reinforcement from Cyclist Base Dpt.	
	13		1 O.R. A.S.C. posted to duty as reinforcement from 2nd Divisional Train.	
			1 O.R's R.A.M.C. despatched for duty to ABBEVILLE for Roads Construction Company	
			1 O.R. A.S.C. H.T. evacuated sick to C.C.S.	
	14		1 O.R's R.A.M.C. evacuated sick to C.C.S.	
	15		3 O.R's R.A.M.C. evacuated sick to C.C.S.	
			3 O.R's A.S.C. H.T. joined for duty as reinforcement from 2nd Divisional Train.	
			2 Nco's 137th Fd.Amb. detach Divisional Rest. you School for 3 days Course of Instruction.	
	16		1 O.R. R.A.M.C. arrived for duty as reinforcement from Base BOULOGNE.	
	17		1 O.R's R.A.M.C. despatched to Transportation Corps Dpts for duty.	
			40th Division R.A.M.C. operation Order No. 19 Copy No 6 received - stating that it is intent of an Advance an Advanced Dressing Station would be opened by these Field Ambulances at CLERY.	
			Headquarters of and in rear of 'HEM'.	

SECRET

Army Form C. 2118.

WAR DIARY
or
INTELLIGENCE SUMMARY

March 1917
Volume X

137th Field Ambulance
R.A.M.C.

Place	Date	Hour	Summary of Events and Information	Remarks and references to Appendices
HEM (Albert Sheet 1/40,000 H8 a.2.7)	18	P.M. 8.30	Verbal orders received from A.D.M.S. to open up a Tent Sub-division and establish an Advanced Dressing Station at CLERY on the 19th inst. NJ	
	19	1	Capt. P.N. EDWARDS, Capt. E.J. YOUNG, Lieut. R.D. MACGREGOR and personnel of Tent Sub-division left HEM for CLERY.	
		4	A.D.S. opened at H6.c.9.5. Sheet 62.c. Capt. J.W. LINNELL and Bearer Squads proceeded to MONT ST. QUENTIN and outskirts of PERONNE and established Advanced Bearer Posts at I 16 a.1.1. and I 21.2.1.1. (Sheet 62E)	
		8	Personnel withdrawn from A.B.P's at P.C. COLONEL — RIVERSIDE — LOCK and MERTON. Verbal orders received from A.D.M.S. to move Headquarters of Field Ambulance from HEM to CLERY on 20 inst. From midnight 19/20 March 19th personal date the Field Ambulance together with 30 O.R's 136th Field Ambulance has been clearing their sick and wounded from 48th Divisional Front (Albert Sheet 1/40,000) Local sick in vicinity of HEM and a Trench Foot Post C 15' d 3.3 to H24 b.5'.0.). Evacuation from the unit: The evacuation from this front line was carried out by horse ambulance wagons from Advanced Bearer Posts situated along the Peronne — Hem and Bran Road at HOWITZER WOOD (Albert Sheet H 3 b.5'.5') were also in charge of this unit. Normal casualties from Regimental Aid Posts and various Advanced Bearer Posts situated along the DECAUVILLE railway running in the valley in squares C 25', B 30, H 6, H5' and H 11 (Albert Sheet 1/40,000). These posts were situated at P.C. MADAME (C25', b.2.5.), VIOLETTE (B 30 central), P.C. MERTON (on GIRDON) (H6 a.3.3.), P.C. COLONEL (H5' a 2.9.), CAR HEAD of CLERY (H 11. A 3.-2.). Two medical officers and 127 O.R's R.A.M.C. were needed at these posts. The country lay intercut and in some parts dangerous. Cases were taken by horses motor lorry ambulances to the Perens rest tents.	

SECRET

Army Form C. 2118.

WAR DIARY
or
INTELLIGENCE SUMMARY.
(Erase heading not required.)

137th Field Ambulance
R.A.M.C.

March 1917
Volume IX

Place	Date	Hour	Summary of Events and Information	Remarks and references to Appendices
HEM	19		Down the valley on track to the Recoundo Ravine as far as Pré-boué CLERY and transferred from L' both Ambulance Cars - by these vehicles to HEM ad MARICOURT (L.L. Main Dressing Station) Putting the cars out on tract at CLERY (H11 a 3.2.) Sen. Aum Keail shelled but only "gas" shells have been evacuated from there. Heavy bright, Memory cases have been sent down during the day to M.D.S of MURREL ALEINE L'.	
Abri/Hut 40,000 H.8.a.27			H10 a 3.5 when Hors./Ambulance Major killed him up and carried him to HEM. In addition L' Post in the valley already received ARP's and starts L' RIVERSIDE (H12 b.77) LOCK (H17 a 6.8) and ants R?A M. BUSCOVET (H16 a 5.5) - No Ambulance or Sulky Bar was left by the last duing the second post on an evacuate B3 cases passed through L' Ophelea Nuring Stations - many of these belonged to t. B A Division. The chann was to Syd J to 40 B Xmas NJ	
	20	10.45 a.m.	Verbal Orders received from A.D.M.S. to open up an Advanced Nuring Station at ALLAINES (62 c. I.4) a twenty. CAPT. E. YOUNG proceeded from CLERY L'MONT ST QUENTIN	
		11 a.m.	Headquarters of Field Ambulance Left HEM to CLERY, Boon Post established in ALLAINES.	
		1 p.m.	Headquarters of unit arrived at CLERY (H6 c 9.8)	
CLERY Shut 62 c (H6 c 9.8)		2	CAPT. P.M. EDWARDS took over Adv. Subdivision Adv. CLERY to ALLAINE S.	

SECRET

Army Form C. 2118.

WAR DIARY
or
INTELLIGENCE SUMMARY.
(Erase heading not required.)

March 1917   Volume X

137th Field Ambulance,
R.A.M.C.

Place	Date	Hour	Summary of Events and Information	Remarks and references to Appendices
CLERY Sht. 62c H 6 c,9,5'	20		Personal withdrawn during the day from A.R.C's at VIOLETTE and MADAME also from RAPs in old British front line. Personnel from HOWITZER WOOD & Garral visit.	
	21	P.M. 4	A.D.S. opened up at ALLAINES (Sheet 62.c I 4 c 2, 3,) Fd.	
			Relay Bearer Post at I 21 c.1.1. withdrawn - Personnel sent to A.R.P I 16 a 1.1.	
		a.m. 9.30	Two motor ambulance cars sent to A.D.S. ALLAINES - great difficulty in getting them nearer to head's load - Roads very bad. Decided to move them and Relay ALLAINES and I 13 c 4.2 - then by one Col. Stitch so horses to H 6 2 9.4. 2/ and form a Car to Lt stretcher bearer Post and motor cars to CLERY A.D.S. Road and bridge CLERY and ALLAINES impassable for motor traffic on tracks.	
		P.M. 2	Ambulance Wagons. 1 NCO & 10 men sent to I 13 2 4.2 to establish a relay Post.	
		P.M. 6	Capts. J.M. LINNELL and YOUNG (officer in chage of A.A.W.) proceeded to Vicinity of BUSSU (J 13) and AIZECOURT - Le - HAUT (J 1) and established dressing posts in those two villages (J 13 c 1.9 and J 1 a 2.2)	
			LIEUT R.D. MACGREGOR temp'y attached as R.M.O. to 12th Bn Yorkshire Regt. (1 N.C.O and 18 men)	
	22	P.M. 2	Relay Bearer Post established at I 12 a 3.3. (ALLAINES - Two motor ambulance wagons sent to A.D.S. ALLAINES -	

WAR DIARY or INTELLIGENCE SUMMARY

Army Form C. 2118.

137th Field Ambulance
R.A.M.C.

March 1917 Volume X

Place	Date	Hour	Summary of Events and Information	Remarks and references to Appendices
CLERY.	23	A.M. 11	Reconnoitred road in vicinity of BUSSU for site for A.D.S. NJ	
H6c9.5"	24	11.35"	40th Divion R.A.M.C. Order No. 21 Copy No 10 Received. — 142nd Divion to if in Northern ALLAINES Sub Sect. Poss'n. 137th Field Ambulance will load one Arnscl Dugout station ALLAINES At a 91.0 and 2nd Station and intchren BUSS Pos'n. MT ST QUENTIN. B4y 4" b/ completed by 2 P.M. March 25.	
(b2c)		12 noon	Orders issued to OC A/S ALLAINES and OC Reserve BUSSU bd AIZECOURT-L-HAUT L'2nd on L H Corp 8th Divion by 2 PM 23rd mil. and prelim. to Hd.of of Arm.W. CLERY.	
		P.M. 1.30	40th Dvn R.A.M.C. Order No 22 Coy No.10 received — 137th Fld Ambulance will proceed from CLERY L' Pont 163 B 14 c. (Central) and be responsible for the evacuation of sick from Hd.S A.L. Rel. area (Aremere L' include LANGSTON Barracks Y LOCK Barracks (SOUTH-AKSNES) ANDOVER PLACE MAGRUER MMS and LITTLESALE BARRACKS. Rem'l to be completed by 6 PM on 23rd inst. Removal of 136th Fd. Amb. attached to this unit to its station at H.Q.on 131 W.A. on I. &t HEM	
		4.30	Orders received from A.D.M.S. to take over from 24th Fd. Amb. P.w. Posts on PINNEYS PNT LE FORGET	
		7.15"	and GRANNIER arrangements made divide into OC 24 Fd Amb. to take over Post at 11 am 25th NJ	
	25	9 am	Post at I 13 & 42 manned afternoon. H/drs taken in CLERY	
			24 Div R.S. Buffs L' Fay over A.R.Ps at PINNEYS PNT, LE FORGET and GRANNIER	

SECRET

WAR DIARY or **INTELLIGENCE SUMMARY**

Army Form C. 2118.

137th Field Ambulance R.A.M.C.

March 1917

Volume X

(Erase heading not required.)

Place	Date	Hour	Summary of Events and Information	Remarks and references to Appendices
CLERY	25	2 P.M.	A.D.S. and Bearer Post at' ALLAINE, BUSSU and AIZECOURT-le-HAUT as well as relieving Bearer Post at I.12 & 3.3. Landed over to 14th Fd. Amb. 8th Division – Personnel Q'mast 137 Ops.	
			F.Amb. at CLERY. 30 O.R's 136th Fd.Amb. (attchd 137th Fd.Amb.) attchd to Bn. units	
		3.15'	Fd.Amb. Hqts CLERY by march moved to Camp 163 MAUREPAS (63C A, oo B 14 C (orthie))	
MAUREPAS Camp 163		5'	Tents arrived at Camp 163. Personal slept in 'h' A.B.P. Bivouac relieved to Fd.Amb. to
63 C 40.00			Fd.Post had already been evacuated by 8th Division. N
B 14 C (orthie)	26	A.M.	CAPT. C.I. YOUNG RAMC deposted to 11th Bn Kings Own Royal Lancashire. Reg't. to medical officers. N
	27	8	Orders received from A.D.M.S. 137 Division to send a tent subdivision (1 officer) to Refugee Camp BRAY.
		Noon	Tent subdivision under CAPT J.W. LINNELL RAMC arrived at Refugee Camp, BRAY.
		12 P.M.	1 N.C.O. & 2 orderly and 1 Water-cart sent to Refugee Camp, BRAY to see tent subdivision was not
		6	found to be sufficient. N
	28	P.M. 6.30	1 officer & 15 O.R's deposted to Refugee Camp, BRAY for duty. N
	29	A.M. 10	LIEUT J. DURDON RAMC & 12 other ranks proceeded to' LE PRIEZ FM. T. GTT. on the Coll'ition from 28th Fd.Amb. & Br.
	31	P.M. 1.30	CAPT L.H. TERRY RAMC reports he arrived for duty – taken on the strength. N
			Orders received from A.D.M.S. to withdraw Personnel from Refugee Camp, BRAY on Midnight. N

N. Malcolm
LIEUT. COLONEL, R.A.M.C.
COMMANDING 137 FIELD AMBULANCE

COMMITTEE FOR THE
MEDICAL HISTORY OF THE WAR
Date -6 JUN. 1917

137th F.A.

SECRET

Army Form C. 2118.

WAR DIARY
or
INTELLIGENCE SUMMARY
(Erase heading not required.)

137th Field Ambulance, R.A.M.C.

April 1917   Volume XI

Place	Date	Hour	Summary of Events and Information	Remarks and references to Appendices
Camp 163 (Ref: 62c) R14.c.central	1	P.M. 5	Order received from A.D.M.S. 40th Division to recconoitre roads and buildings in the vicinity of MOISLAINS with a view to the move of the Fd. Amb. to that place in the near future.	
	2	P.M. 1.45	CAPT. J.W. LINNELL, R.A.M.C. and party returned from Nurses Camp, BRAY. Rode to MOISLAINS – found that road between MOISLAINS and BOUCHAVESNES is impassable to transport. Road between MOISLAINS and CLERY and HAUT ALLAINES in good order. Accomodation for a Field Ambulance in MOISLAINS is very bad.	
	3	P.M. 5	Reconnd. di PINNEY'S POST, LE FOREST and LE PRIEZ Fm. relieved by No.1, 7 mn. firm. Hd.Qrs. of Fd. Amb.	
	4	P.M. 7	40th Division R.A.M.C. Order No. 23 Copy No. 11 received stating that 137th Field Ambulance are on the "int. division" will move to MOISLAINS on 7th April and will be responsible for the collection and evacuation of sick and wounded from the Divisional Front area. Advance parties will be not' formal to establish Field site. VICKERS to supply to MOISLAINS. On the "I - sub division" (on the "II - ") to run a Relieving Station. Hot- and Rest A'- EARLY. The medical inspection Rms. to be open as customary of 6th mls.	
		10.15	Order received from A.D.M.S. L' and 3 hrs. Ambulance Cars to 2nd Fd. Amb. at A.17.C.C.U.P. as the 8th Division had suffered heavy casualties.	

T2134. Wt. W708-776. 500000. 4/15. Sir J. C. & S.

WAR DIARY or INTELLIGENCE SUMMARY

Army Form C. 2118.

(Erase heading not required.)

SECRET

Volume XI — 37 Field Ambulance RAMC

April 1917

Place	Date	Hour	Summary of Events and Information	Remarks and references to Appendices
Camp 163	4	10.30 PM	2 large ambulance cars and 1 2nd ambulance car despatched to 24 Fd. Amb.	
	5	10 AM	Cars returned from 24th Field Ambulance. The unit having been relieved by 24th Ambulance Convoy.	
		5.40 PM	Instructions received from A.D.M.S. to send a M.O. for temporary duty with 21st Divisional M.V.	
		1	Instructions received from A.D.M.S. on arrival at MOISLAINS to take ambulance wagon to L.Bn. Hd. for temporary duty & 135 Fd. Amb. Casualties evacuated by 135 Fd. Amb. will be sent to 137 Fd. Amb. for further evacuation to RY Rev. Amb. Train at POZIERES Station via 21st Middle Ry.	
	6	2	CAPT. L.H. TERRY, R.A.M.C. proceeded for temporary duty with 21st Middle Ry.	
		4	CAPT. J.N. LINNELL, R.A.M.C. and 1 Tent subdivision + 6 R.A.M.C. other ranks on duty L.B.T.G. CIRLU proceeded to LINGER CAMP to establish Medical Inspection Room to 123 Infantry RH.	
		9 AM	Advanced Retention Hut and Medical Inspection Hut opened at LINGER CAMP CURLU.	
		6 PM	Transport of unit under LIEUT. J. DUNDON R.A.M.C. left for MOISLAINS via GUERY.	
MOISLAINS Sheet 62 C (40,100) C 12.c.7.7	7	1.45 AM	R.A.M.C. personnel of unit left for MOISLAINS via LE FORRET, RANCOURT, BOUCHAVESNES.	
		5	R.A.M.C. personnel arrived at MOISLAINS – opened up Medical Inspection Room. Personnel established in cellars and rooms.	
	8	9 AM	LIEUT. J. DUNDON R.A.M.C. proceeded for temp. duty as M.O. i/c 21st Divl. R.V. vice CAPT. L.H. TERRY R.A.M.C. posted to duty at No. 5 C.C.S. – Lower off the strength.	

SECRET

Army Form C. 2118.

Instructions regarding War Diaries and Intelligence
Summaries are contained in F. S. Regs., Part II.
and the Staff Manual respectively. Title pages
will be prepared in manuscript.

WAR DIARY
or
INTELLIGENCE SUMMARY.
(Erase heading not required.)

Volume XI 137th Field Ambulance
April 1917 R.A.M.C.

Place	Date	Hour	Summary of Events and Information	Remarks and references to Appendices
MOISLAINS	14		2 O.Rs. deputed for duty at A.D.C.C.S. and Admonition Committee at Abbey Raillais respectively.	
	15	P.M.	Order received from A.D.M.S. to withdraw Personnel from Baths and Isolation Hospital, CURLU on 16th inst.	
	16	4.30	CAPT. J.W. LINNELL and party returned from CURLU. During the 9 days the Isolation Hospital was	
			open — 231 patients were admitted.	
			Admissions O.Rs Sick 26	
	17		Admissions O.Rs Sick 4	
	18		Admissions O.Rs Sick 3 LIEUT. R.D. MACGREGOR, R.A.M.C. posted to permanent duty with 12th Br.	
	19		Gurkha Regt. and struck off the strength. CAPT. F.G. THATCHER R.A.M.C. temporarily attached for duty	
			from 135th Field Ambulance.	
	20		Admissions O.Rs Sick 6. CAPT. J.S. BEVERIDGE, R.A.M.C. admitted to H.Qrs. from to 6 General Hospital	
	21		Admissions O.Rs Sick 5.	
	22		Admissions O.Rs Sick 3. CAPT. J.S. BEVERIDGE, R.A.M.C. detailed for temporary duty to M.2 1/2 181st R.G. R.F.A.	
	23		Admissions O.Rs Sick 6.	
		12.15 P.M.	40th Division R.A.M.C. Operation Order No. 24 copy No. 11 received — 137th Fd. Amb. (less 1 Tent Subdivision	
			and 1 officer) to proceed to MANANCOURT and open up Nursing Station by 6 P.M. 23-4-17.	
MANANCOURT (37C d.9.a) V.13 a.9.4.		5'	Unit (less 1 Tent Subdivision and 1 officer) arrived at MANANCOURT and took over buildings & site from 136 Fd Amb	

SECRET

Army Form C. 2118.

137th Field Ambulance
R.A.M.C.

WAR DIARY
or
INTELLIGENCE SUMMARY.
(Erase heading not required.)

Volume XI
April 1917

Place	Date	Hour	Summary of Events and Information	Remarks and references to Appendices
MANANCOURT	23	PM 10	Orders (verbal) received from A.D.M.S. to send 1 Officer and 1 Bearer Sub-division to 136th Field Amb. FINS. Under instructions from O.C. 136th Fd. Amb. CAPT. THATCHER, R.A.M.C. and 1 Bearer Sub-division with Water, Blanket, and hot water-cart, proceeded to FINS.	
			Admissions O.R's Sick 31.	
	24	PM 6	Orders received from A.D.M.S. to send 1 Officer and 1 Bearer Sub-division to "136th" Amb. O.C. 136th Fd. Amb. FINS notified delay.	
	25	7.15	CAPT. P.M. EDWARDS, R.A.M.C. and 2 Bearer Sub-division left to FINS.	
			Admissions Officers Sick 2, O.R's Sick 45.	
		AM 8	Divisional Baths under control of Field Ambulance, opened at ETRICOURT	
		Noon 12	Soup Kitchen & Rest House under control of Field Ambulance, opened at MOISLAINS	
			Admissions Officers Sick 2, O.R's Sick 14.	
	26		Admissions O.R's Sick 20. LIEUT J. DUNDON, R.A.M.C. returned to duty from 21st Fd Amb. Capt.	
	27		2 O.R's R.A.M.C. despatched to duty as Medical Orderlies with XV Corps Ammunition Park, CURLU	
			Admissions O.R's Sick 13. Under instructions from A.D.M.S. Soup Kitchen & Rest House at MOISLAINS	
	28	NT 12	handed over to "A" CAPT. J.W. GIBSON, R.A.M.C. M.O. i/c "A" Divisional (Amb.). 6 O.R's R.A.M.C. remain for duty with this office. CAPT. J.W. LINNELL and the Tent sub-division (less 6 O.R's) returned to its Fd. Amb. for duty.	

SECRET

Army Form C. 2118.

137th Field Ambulance
R.A.M.C.

WAR DIARY
or
INTELLIGENCE SUMMARY.
(Erase heading not required.)

Volume X
April 1917

Instructions regarding War Diaries and Intelligence Summaries are contained in F. S. Regs., Part II. and the Staff Manual respectively. Title pages will be prepared in manuscript.

Place	Date	Hour	Summary of Events and Information	Remarks and references to Appendices
MANANCOURT	28	4 PM	1 N.C.O. arrived as N-inferior from 7th Guards Entrenching Battalion.	
	29	5 PM	Admissions O.R's Sick 16. 29 O.R's 137th F.Amb. returned from A.D.S. METZ-EN-COUTURE having completed duty as Bearers with 136th Field Ambulance.	
	30		Admissions O.R's Sick 23. During the month of April 835 patients treated at Field Ambulance and returned to "duty" — these also not include patients transferred to Corps Main Dressing Station, evacuated to C.C.S or admitted to Field Ambulance — they were "out-patients". The Field Ambulance during the month has been treating the men of units without a Medical Officer and details of units whose M.O. was not in Battalion at line. During the month 6 O.R's of the Field Ambulance have been evacuated sick to C.C.S / temporary vacancies. The work in all April 22 OC's R.A.M.C. In charge.	

[signature]
LIEUT. COLONEL, R.A.M.C.
COMMANDING 137 FIELD AMBULANCE.

May 1917 40 Div 14/2/61

No 137. F.A.

COMMITTEE FOR THE
MEDICAL HISTORY OF THE WAR
Date   10 JUL. 1917

Army Form C. 2118.

SECRET

Instructions regarding War Diaries and Intelligence
Summaries are contained in F. S. Regs., Part II.
and the Staff Manual respectively. Title pages
will be prepared in manuscript.

WAR DIARY
or
INTELLIGENCE SUMMARY.
(Erase heading not required.)

137th Field Ambulance.
R.A.M.C.

Volume XII
May, 1917

Vol 12

Place	Date	Hour	Summary of Events and Information	Remarks and references to Appendices
MANANCOURT (Sheet 57C 1/40,000) V.13.a.9.4.	1		Admissions OR's SicR 23	
	2		Admissions OR's SicR 20	
	3		Admissions OR's Wounded 1 Sick Officers 1 OR's 18	
		PM 10.30	Gas alarm sounded by standing forms in vicinity. All precautions taken - patients washed and eyes	
			irrigated, held in readiness. No gas cases seen.	
		10.30	R.A.M.C. Operation Order (40th Division) No 25 copy to 11 received - stating that the 40th Division will stand	
			to 25 lefty. Operation order to 3rd Division on the 5th Army zero hour will be 10.30 PM -	
			LA VACQUERIE position in conjunction with the 2nd Division on the 3rd Army.	
			137th Field Ambulance will attack 3 hours subdivision to 136th Field Ambulance on the 4th mil.	
	4	AM 10	Admissions OR's Wounded 3 SicR 11	
			Order received from A.D.M.S. 40th Division that Operation Order No 25 dated 3/5/17 is in abeyance.	
		Noon 12	Verbal Order received from A.D.M.S. that Operation Order No 25 dated 3/5/17 now holds good with the	
			exception that the nature of the operation will be a raid instead of an attempt to capture and	
			hold LA VACQUERIE	
		PM 4.30	CAPT J.W.LINNELL, LIEUT. J DUNDEN and 65 O.R's 137th F.Amb. proceeded by march route to FINS "A"	
			& "B" OC 136th Field Ambulance (on bearer subdivision is already attached to "A" unit and "A" & "B"	
			of "A"ville to send two other complete "bearer sub divisions to "B" unit and to remit the "C" permit.)	

SECRET

Army Form C. 2118.

WAR DIARY
or
INTELLIGENCE SUMMARY.
(Erase heading not required.)

Volume XII

137th Field Ambulance R.A.M.C.

May 1917

Place	Date	Hour	Summary of Events and Information	Remarks and references to Appendices
MANANCOURT	5	P.M. 4.30	Admissions O.R's Wounded 1 Sick 26	
			1 O.R. 137th Field Ambulance killed in action near METZ-EN-COUTURE.	
			This is the first battle casualty in the unit. 20 '13.R' was wounded on night 24/25 April near	
			VILLERS PLOUICH	
	6		Admissions O.R's Sick 5. During last two days the only Medical Officer at the H.Q. of	
			the Field Ambulance has been the O.C. – The A.D.M.S. has detailed the M.O/C 4th S.W. A.S.C. and	
			the M.O/C 40th Div. Amm. Col. to attend at Dressing Station at 9 a.m. & see admissions were	
			Average number of such attendances is 120. - None of the men are suffering from trench disease, ideas	
			feet, lip and hand. At least 300 dressings are applied during the day. There are 75 patients	
			detained in this Nursing Station. Two wards are in old stables. Two operating tents and two	
			bell tents are in use as wards. Owing to the late hr. 25' received in to 3rd week to	
			staff of the Nursing Station has been reduced to a minimum – 35' O.R.'s (including Clerks	
			Cooks Car orderlies Nursing orderlies Store-men etc.)	
		P.M. 6.30	LIEUT. J. DUNDON returned to H.Q. from duty with 136th 2nd Ambl. FINS	
		8.30	CAPT. F.G. THATCHER returned to Fd. Gen. from duty with 136. 2d Ambl. at A.D.S. METZ-EN-COUTURE,	
		11.50	3/6 O.R's 137th 2d Ambl. returned to Fd. Gen. from duty with 136th 2d Ambl. FINS	

SECRET

Army Form C. 2118.

Instructions regarding War Diaries and Intelligence Summaries are contained in F.S. Regs., Part II. and the Staff Manual respectively. Title pages will be prepared in manuscript.

WAR DIARY or INTELLIGENCE SUMMARY

(Erase heading not required.)

Volume XII

137th Field Ambulance, R.A.M.C.

May 1917

Place	Date	Hour	Summary of Events and Information	Remarks and references to Appendices
MANANCOURT	7		Admission O.R's Sick 11. CAPT. F.G. THATCHER, R.A.M.C. reported for duty on return R.A.M.S. 40th Division. CAPT. F.W. EDWARDS, R.A.M.C. and 2 P.Os. returned from duty with 138th Fd. Amb. at A.D.S. METZ-EN-COUTURE.	
	8		Admission O.R's Sick 6. Wounded 1. CAPT. J.W. BINGHAM, R.A.M.C. came to relieve CAPT. P.G. FAULKES. M.O. i/c 178th Bde. R.F.A. - The latter officer taken on the strength of this unit. 6 P.Os. returned to duty from 136th Fd. Amb.	
	9		Admission O.R's Wounded 2. Sick 14.	
	10		Admissions O.R's Sick 11. CAPT. A.J. BEVERIDGE, R.A.M.C. returned to duty from XX Corps Laundry.	
	11		Admissions O.R's Wounded 1. Sick 13. The officers and an N.C.O. attended lectures and demonstration on the fitting of gas helmets at Divnl. School FINS - Subjects of lectures and demonstration - The fitting of gas helmets at Divnl. School FINS - Subjects of lectures and demonstration - The fitting of gas helmets et.	
		P.M. 6.30	40th Division R.A.M.C. operation order No. 26 copy No 11 received. The Corps front will be reorganized. 20th Division to take over front held by left Brigade of 8th Division. 8th Division front to be taken over by two Brigades of 40th Division i.e. 3 Brigades of 40th Division on to line. 137th Field Ambulance (less sufficient personnel to run a detention hospital at MANANCOURT and huts et. ETRICOURT) will move from MANANCOURT to HEUDICOURT on 14.5.13 and take over Nissen hut and Bearer Pols. from 24th Field Ambulance 8th Division and to reorganize	

SECRET

Army Form C. 2118.

WAR DIARY or INTELLIGENCE SUMMARY
(Erase heading not required.)

137th Field Ambulance
R.A.M.C.
Volume XII
May 1917

Place	Date	Hour	Summary of Events and Information	Remarks and references to Appendices
MANANCOURT	12		On the evacuation of sick and wounded from the Rifle Brigade Stab of relief to be arranged between O.C.'s concerned.	
		A.M. 7	CAPT. Q.J. BEVERIDGE, R.A.M.C. and 23 O.R's proceeded for duty with 135th Fd. Amb.	
		9	Proceeded my with CAPT. P.W. EDWARDS to HEUDICOURT and interviewed O.C. A.D.S. at that place with a view to taking over. Proceeded to Advanced Bearer Post at YVRECELETTE FM. and VILLERS GUISLAIN and R.A.P.'s in that area. Arranged to send an officer with advanced party to take over – party to march on evening 13th and Posts to be relieved early 14th inst.	
	13	P.M. 11.30	CAPT. J.W. LINNELL, R.A.M.C. and 39 O.R's returned from duty with 135th Fd. Amb.	
			Admissions Sur. Officer 1 O.R 12	
			Admissions O.R's Sur. 21	
		P.M. 4.30	CAPT. P.W. EDWARDS and 30 O.R's proceeded by march route to HEUDICOURT. (No. 137 C)	
			40,000	
			Admissions O.R's Sur. 13	
	14	P.M. 3	Field Ambulance (less park) with 136th Fd. Amb., One Advanced party less 18 O.R's left for duty at Motor hospital MANANCOURT under CAPT. J.W. LINNELL) proceeded to HEUDICOURT.	

SECRET

Army Form C. 2118.

WAR DIARY
or
INTELLIGENCE SUMMARY.
(Erase heading not required.)

Volume XII

137th Field Ambulance, R.A.M.C.

May 1917

Place	Date	Hour	Summary of Events and Information	Remarks and references to Appendices
HEUDICOURT (Sh. 57c 1/40,000) N.21.c.3.9.	14th	P.M. 7	Main party of unit arrived at HEUDICOURT. Building of A.D.S. and Bearer Posts had already been taken over now from 24th Fd. Amb. Advanced Bearer Post at X 13 c 2.0 and X 9 c 0.7 - the latter in a cellar. Personnel 1 NCO and 4 men at each. Personnel 2" and 3rd " 1 NCO and 4 men at . Walled stretchers, surgical haversacks & Medical comforts, Flasks, shell dressings.	I. Scheme of evacuation and nof.
	15th		Wounded brought from R.A.P's (3) by tramp bearers. Schemes of evacuation and map attached (I) (No) Admissions Wounded OR's 1, Sick Officers 2 OR's 28. As wounded except stretcher cases go for direct-evacuation to CCS on admission to the Field Ambulance - all other to advance to XVth Corps Main Nursery Station, FINS (V.18.c). B.i.R on T.2.T at Admission LIEUT. J. DUNDIN, R.A.M.C. sent to temporary duty as M.O. Y.c. M.T.Star Bn. R.E. on Camp 2.0 (MARICOURT)	
	16th	P.M. 2	Admissions Sick OR's 17. CAPT. J.O's. BEVERIDGE returned to duty from 181st Bde. R.F.A. Activities received from A.S.M.S as to existence of new Imperial Trench. Map refs. X17d95; X.16c47: X.199.00. N.29d.00. E.10.a.a.8.(a.not) Nemir. R3645; R325d15.7 Sunk.Rd. X.23.k.4.2. X.24.a.9. X.24.c.18. Trench RAILTON (No58)	
		6	Rifle Brigade Pandemic — Personnel at Advanced Bearer Post (DC 9 C 0.7) increased by six bearers. Admission Officers Sick 1 OR's Sick 23.	
	17th 18th		Admissions Officers Sick 1 OR's Sick 27.	

SECRET

Army Form C. 2118.

WAR DIARY
or
INTELLIGENCE SUMMARY.
(Erase heading not required.)

Army XII / 137th Field Ambulance, R.A.M.C.

Nov 1917

Place	Date	Hour	Summary of Events and Information	Remarks and references to Appendices
HEUDICOURT	19th		Admission O.R's Sick 8.	
	20.		Admission Officers Sick 1, O.R's Sick 14 Wounded 1.	
		P.M. 2	40th Division R.A.M.C. Operation Order No. 27 Copy No. 11 received — 38th Division will take over the portion of the line now held by 119, 120, 121 and 120th Infantry Brigade. 137th Field Ambulance will hand over on the 23rd inst. to 106th Field Ambulance. 33rd Division to Dressing Station at HEUDICOURT and Bearer Post at X.13.c.2.1. and X.9.c.9.8. and return to its old site at MANANCOURT and to responsible for the collection of sick from the Divisional Rear Area in " of FINS.	
		2.15	Officer commanding 106th Field Ambulance arrived to make arrangements for taking over the duties of this command. 106th Field Ambulance will send one section of the unit to proceed to the Dressing Station on 23rd inst. N1., the remainder to 21st inst. N1.".	
	21st		Admission O.R's Sick 19.	
		noon 12	Intimation received from A.D.M.S. that 121st "Infantry" Brigade are making a raid on BISQUET FARM X.18.a.8.4. and HONNECOURT WOOD X.11.d after "midnight" tonight. There may be a considerable number of casualties.	
		P.M. 2	2 Officers and 1 Section 106th Field Ambulance arrived as advanced party.	
		7	8 O.R's sent to Advanced Bearer Post (4 to cart) — extra blankets, stretchers, medical comforts sent	

SECRET

Volume XII

Army Form C. 2118.

Instructions regarding War Diaries and Intelligence Summaries are contained in F.S. Regs., Part II. and the Staff Manual respectively. Title pages will be prepared in manuscript.

WAR DIARY
or
INTELLIGENCE SUMMARY

137th Field Ambulance, R.A.M.C.

May 1917

(Erase heading not required.)

Place	Date	Hour	Summary of Events and Information	Remarks and references to Appendices
HEUDICOURT	21		Drivers sent to these posts. A second driving room equipped at this Dressing Station – extra night duties warned.	
		P.M. 8.30	1 Lewis Motor Ambulance Car and 1 Ford car with M.T. N.C.O. and 1 L. R.B.P's "A" reported to Firm cars wheel at these posts.	
	22		Admissions Officers Lieut 1 O.R.; Lieut 23 Wounded 2. 1 Officer 3 O.R's and 1 wounded German prisoner passed through the A.D.S. during the night – casualties "Nicol" & Read.	
		A.M. 10	40th Division R.A.M.C. operation orders No. 28 copy 11 received – this O/C cancels O.O. 27 with the inception of the move of this Unit.	
	23	A.M. 6	Advanced Bearer Posts at D.C.9 C.0.7 and D.C.13 C.2.0. handed over to 105" Fd Amb.	
		9	Dressing Station HEUDICOURT handed over to 106th Fd Amb.	
		9.15	Unit marched out to MANANCOURT.	
MANANCOURT		11.50	Fd Amb arrived at MANANCOURT.	
V13 a 9.4. (Sheet 57C)			Admissions O.R's Lieut 23.	
	24		During the period May 14 – 23, only 2 officers and 27 O.R's (Wounded) passed Through Dressing Station at HEUDICOURT.	
			Admission O.R's Lieut 12.	

Volume XII.

SECRET

Army Form C. 2118.

WAR DIARY
or
INTELLIGENCE SUMMARY.
(Erase heading not required.)

Army Form C. 2118.

137th Field Ambulance
R.E.A.S.

May 1917

Instructions regarding War Diaries and Intelligence Summaries are contained in F. S. Regs., Part II. and the Staff Manual respectively. Title pages will be prepared in manuscript.

Place	Date	Hour	Summary of Events and Information	Remarks and references to Appendices
MANANCOURT	25		Admission O.R's Sick 13	
	26		Admission O.R's Sick 3	
		9.30 a.m.	2 O.R's 137th Field Ambulance Report for duty at XVth Corps School, DAOURS	
	27		Admission O.R's Sick 13	
		1 p.m.	Conversation with A.D.M.S. re medical arrangements of 40th Division on and after 29th inst. 137th F.A. and to take over Butts at SOREL and the Field Ambulance Station are Butts at NURLU on the 29th May. Butts at ETRICOURT to be handed on to Town troops of Tank phase. 1 Tank Field division 12 horses and 2 officers with equipment and the Horse and Tank over from 24th Fd. Amb. NURLU on 29th inst.	
		4.30	Visited NURLU interviewed O.C. 24th Fd. Amb. and arranged to hand over to them on 28th inst. at 6 P.M.	
	28		Admissions O.R's Sick 8	
		10.20 A.M.	Medical arrangements 40th Division Copy No. 8 received – 137th Field Ambulance Headquarters MANANCOURT and one Tent Subdivision at NURLU will be responsible for the evacuation of sick from the Divisional Back Area from FINS exclusive. Two officers, one Tent Subdivision 12 bearers, transport etc. provided by NURLU.	
		4.30		

SECRET

Army Form C. 2118.

WAR DIARY
or
INTELLIGENCE SUMMARY

Volume XII

137th Field Ambulance
R.A.M.C.

May 1917

(Erase heading not required.)

Instructions regarding War Diaries and Intelligence Summaries are contained in F. S. Regs., Part II. and the Staff Manual respectively. Title pages will be prepared in manuscript.

Place	Date	Hour	Summary of Events and Information	Remarks and references to Appendices
MANANCOURT	29		Admission O.R's Sick 11	
	30		Admission O.R's Sick 22	
		4.25 P.M.	Instructions re Medical arrangements 40th Division dated 28/5/17 received. The Tent subdivision of 137th Field Ambulance NUREU will be reponsible for collection of sick from Medical Inspection Room NUREU from May 30 inclusive.	
	31		Admission O.R's Sick 21.	
			Orders received from A.D.M.S. to send daily a Medical Officer to sort of 311th Roads Contruction Company, RANCOURT, commencing June 1.	

R Murdoch
LIEUT. COLONEL,
R.A.M.C.
COMMANDING 137 FIELD AMBULANCE

T2134. Wt. W708–776. 500000. 4/15. Sir J. C. & S.

Appendix I

Scheme of Evacuation from Right Brigade

Place	Map Reading	Personnel	Accommodation
H.Q. & Dressing Stn.	57C W 21. b 3. 9	—	50 Patients
Bearer Post	X. 13. c. 2.0	1 NCO + 4 men	—
do	X. 9. c. 0. 7	do	—

Cases are brought by hand or wheeled stretcher from the 3 R. A. P. in X. 9. a (Sheet 57C 1/40000) to the Bearer Post at X. 9. C. 0. 7.

During the day, serious cases are brought on wheeled stretchers to the Bearer Post at X. 13. C. 2. 0, a distance of about 2,000 yds, but during the night, a Ford Motor Ambulance Car, proceeds from the Head Quarters at W21. b. 3. 9 to the Bearer Post at X. 9. C. 0. 7 and removes all cases to the Post at X. 13. C. 2. 0, within 50 yards of which Post is the Regimental Aid Post of the Battalion in Reserve.

At the latter Bearer Post, i.e. the one at X. 13. C. 2. 0, a large car is stationed day and night, & is used to evacuate all cases to the Dressing Station at HEUDICOURT — W. 21. b. 3. 9.

Cases on arrival at the Dressing Station are dealt with as follows:-

(1) Sick cases that are likely to recover quickly, are detained here and treated.
(2) All other cases are sent to the XV. Corps Main Dressing Station at FINS, by Horsed Ambulances and Cars.
(3) Seriously wounded cases are evacuated direct to C.C.S at PERONNE

The Morning sick of details etc. in HEUDICOURT, are

Appendix I

also seen at this Dressing Station, and cases requiring attention and rest are detained.

A.C.Anderton
Lieut Colonel RAMC
Commanding 137 Field Ambulance

COMMITTEE FOR THE
MEDICAL HISTORY OF THE WAR

Date -7 AUG.1917

No. 187. 7a

June 1917.

SECRET

Army Form C. 2118.

WAR DIARY
or
INTELLIGENCE SUMMARY.
(Erase heading not required.)

Instructions regarding War Diaries and Intelligence Summaries are contained in F. S. Regs., Part II. and the Staff Manual respectively. Title pages will be prepared in manuscript.

Volume 13 June 1917

137th Field Ambulance R.A.M.C.

Vol 13

Place	Date	Hour	Summary of Events and Information	Remarks and references to Appendices
MANANCOURT (Sheet 57 C 1/40,000 V 13 a 94)	1		Admission O.R's SurR 18.	
			CAPT. P.G. FOULKES R.A.M.C. detached for Temporary duty with 136th Field Ambulance.	
	2		Admission O.R's SurR 22.	
	3	P.M.	Admission O.R's SurR 21.	
		3'	Two NCO's left to attend class of instruction at 40th Divisional Gas School FINS.	
		11.30	Gas alarm sounded. All precautions taken - patients prepared. Gas did not reach the village.	
			1 NCO and 10 pts. Sed. "L" 3rd Corps than Nequay Station to Temporary duty in working parts.	
			LIEUT. J. DUNDON, R.A.M.C. returned from duty with 12th Labour Bn. R.E.	
	4		Admission Officers SurR 2 O.R's SurR 22.	
	5		Admission O.R's SurR 14.	
			Copy of medical arrangements "3rd Corps received.	
			Admission O.R's SurR 28.	
	6		CAPT. H.R. POLLOCK R.A.M.C. returned from 4th Army School of Musketry, PONT REMY and transferred to 136th Field Ambulance.	
	7		Admission O.R's SurR 20. As previously send for duty with 13th Balloon Company R.F.C.; NCO qualified as "out" as confirmed gas NCO's.	
			2 NCO's returned from Gas School FINS - both qualified as "out" as confirmed gas NCO's.	

SECRET

Army Form C. 2118.

Instructions regarding War Diaries and Intelligence Summaries are contained in F.S. Regs., Part II. and the Staff Manual respectively. Title pages will be prepared in manuscript.

WAR DIARY
or
INTELLIGENCE SUMMARY

Volume 13
137th Field Ambulance. R.A.M.C.
June 1917

(Erase heading not required.)

Place	Date	Hour	Summary of Events and Information	Remarks and references to Appendices
MANANCOURT	8	A.M. 2	Admissions. O.R's Sick 18. Gas alarm. Patients and personnel warned and prepared. No gas reached the village.	
	9	A.M. 9	Admissions. O.R's Sick 12. 4 ptes. 43rd Divisional Employment Company reported for duty. Two of them on posta "L". The Batn. of NURLU and Two L" the Batn at SOREL. From pte. 137th Fd Amb. Withdrawn from the Battn.	
"	10		Admissions. O.R's Sick 24. 1 Sgt. and 1 private detached for topog. duty at 3rd Corps Bombards. Depot, GEESY.	
"	11		Admissions. O.R's Sick 19. 1 N.C.O. detailed for personnel duty at D.19 Advanced Depot. Medical Store PERONNE – LA – CHAPELETTE. Strength of the strength.	
"	12		1 Pte. deputised to duty as Dental Orderly 4th Army Dental Orly. PERONNE. 1 Pte. transferred to 40th Divisional Employment Company. Labour Corps. 2 O.R's transferred to XVth Corps Infantry School.	
"	19		Capt. J. JARDINE R.A.M.C. posted to duty from 136th Field Ambulance – taken on the strength and detached for duty with XVth Corps Headquarters.	

SECRET.

Army Form C. 2118.

WAR DIARY
or
INTELLIGENCE SUMMARY
(Erase heading not required.)

Volume 13
June 1917

137th Field Ambulance, R.A.M.C.

Place	Date	Hour	Summary of Events and Information	Remarks and references to Appendices
MANANCOURT	20		1 Sergt. R.A.M.C. reported for duty from 36 C.C.S. — taken on strength.	
	22		CAPT. J. JARDINE, R.A.M.C. posted to 32nd Division and struck off the strength.	
	23		1 Corpl. and 9 Pte. R.A.M.C. reported for duty from Eyebris Base Depot — taken on strength.	
	24		LIEUT. C.J. BUCKLEY, United States Medical Corps posted to unit for duty and taken on strength.	
	25		1 Pte. despatched to duty with "C" Corps Ammunition Park, A.S.C. and struck off strength.	
	26		1 Pte. returned to duty from 41 Stationary Hospital.	
	29		Verbal instructions received from A.D.M.S. 40th Div. to hold the unit in readiness to relieve 21. And of 35th Division at HEUDICOURT	
	30	A.M. 9.15	40th Division R.A.M.C. Operation Orders No 29 reply No 10 received:— 137th Field Ambulance Hdqrs. will move to HEUDICOURT on 3rd July leaving on tent sub-division (Mess one officer) at MANANCOURT and NURLU until further orders. They will take over from 106th Field Ambulance, 35th Division the Main Dressing Station at HEUDICOURT, and the Advanced Dressing Station at VILLERS GUISLAIN and will be responsible for the collection of sick and wounded from Right Brigade, and from Divisional front area excluding FINS. Relief is to completed by 12 noon 3rd July. 106th Field Ambulance 35th Division will evacuate sick and wounded of 121st Infantry Brigade until 12 noon 3rd July.	

SECRET.

Army Form C. 2118.

WAR DIARY
or
INTELLIGENCE SUMMARY.
(Erase heading not required.)

Volume 13
June 1917
137th Field Ambulance R.A.M.C.

Instructions regarding War Diaries and Intelligence Summaries are contained in F.S. Regs., Part II. and the Staff Manual respectively. Title pages will be prepared in manuscript.

Place	Date	Hour	Summary of Events and Information	Remarks and references to Appendices
MANANCOURT	30	P.M. 2	Accompanied by CAPT. J.W. LINNELL, R.A.M.C. and O.C. No.10 Light Railway operating R.E. proceeded by Decauville Railway from FINS to CHAPEL CROSSING (near VILLERS GUISLAIN) and made arrangements for evacuation of sick and wounded by Decauville to Carpe Nau Railway Station. FINS from VILLERS GUISLAIN and HEUDICOURT. Saw O.C. 106th Field Ambulance and arranged for send advanced parties to VILLERS GUISLAIN and HEUDICOURT on 2nd July.	
		4.30	121st Infantry Brigade Orders No. 109 Copy No. 27 received. The Brigade will relieve 33rd Division on nights 1/2 July, 2/3 July. Since 12th instant, 4 officers 275 O.Rs sick have been admitted to this Field Ambulance. In addition 1 wounded escaped Russian prisoner was admitted on 18th inst. and 1 wounded German prisoner was admitted on 24th inst. Both of these were evacuated to C.C.S. During the month 2028 sick and slightly wounded cases were treated in this Field Ambulance and returned to duty — This includes "hearing sick".	

[signature]
LIEUT. COLONEL,
R.A.M.C.
COMMANDING 137 FIELD AMBULANCE

No. 137. 7.a.

COMMITTEE FOR THE
MEDICAL HISTORY OF THE WAR
Date 10 SEP. 1917

Army Form C. 2118.

SECRET

Instructions regarding War Diaries and Intelligence
Summaries are contained in F.S. Regs., Part II.
and the Staff Manual respectively. Title pages
will be prepared in manuscript.

WAR DIARY
or
INTELLIGENCE SUMMARY
(Erase heading not required.)

137ᵗʰ Field Ambulance, R.A.M.C.

Volume XIV
July 1917

√51/14

Place	Date	Hour	Summary of Events and Information	Remarks and references to Appendices
MANANCOURT (Sheet 57C 40/000 V13a94)	2	P.M. 3	14 O.R's 137ᵗʰ Fd. Amb. returned from 136ᵗʰ Fd. Amb.	
			Advance party consisting of CAPT. J.N. LINNELL, R.A.M.C., LIEUT. C.J. BUCKLEY, M.S.R.C. and 29 O.R's R.A.M.C. left for HEUDICOURT and VILLERS GUISLAIN.	
			LIEUT. J. DUNDON, R.A.M.C. struck off strength - having been permitted to relinquish his Commission.	
	3	A.M. 10	CAPT. P.G. FOULKES, R.A.M.C. returned from duty with 136ᵗʰ Fd. Amb.	
			Field Ambulance Coll: Stretchers at NURLU (in Adv. park) HEUDICOURT and VILLERS GUISLAIN.	
			Lieut. CAPT. P.G. FOULKES and 14 O.R's remaining at MANANCOURT, proceeded by road into "HEUDICOURT.	see App. I
HEUDICOURT (Sheet 57C 40/000 h/21.2.39)		Noon 12	Bearer Posts Advanced Dressing Station and Hd. Qrs. Field Ambulance taken over from 106ᵗʰ Fd. Amb. 33ʳᵈ Division -	
			Took over Medical and Sanitary charge of the Battalion of 121ᵗʰ Bde. in reserve - two bns. at VAUCELETTE	
			Fm. and two Brgs. at HEUDICOURT.	
			Took over Baths at HEUDICOURT.	
	4	P.M. 6	2 O.R's proceeded for duty with Town Major, HARBONNIERS.	
			2 O.R's returned from duty with 136ᵗʰ Field Ambulance	
	5	A.M. 10	Hd. Division passed under command of Third Army.	
		P.M. 6	6 O.R's returned from duty with 136ᵗʰ Field Ambulance	
	6	Noon 12	1 Officer and 14 O.R's withdrawn from MANANCOURT - Attention Hospital closed - buildings handed over to L'Town Major.	

SECRET

Army Form C. 2118.

Instructions regarding War Diaries and Intelligence
Summaries are contained in F. S. Regs., Part II.
and the Staff Manual respectively. Title pages
will be prepared in manuscript.

WAR DIARY
or
INTELLIGENCE SUMMARY.
(Erase heading not required.)

Volume XIV
July 1917

137ᴬ Field Ambulance, R.A.M.C.

Place	Date	Hour	Summary of Events and Information	Remarks and references to Appendices
HEUDICOURT	7	P.M. 6	11 O.R's R.A.M.C. returned from duty at 3rd Corps Main Dressing Station (V 18 c.)	
	8	P.M. 2	1 Pte R.A.M.C. returned from duty at Water Point, CRANIERE	
			40ᵗʰ Division R.A.M.C. Operation Order No 30. Copy No 11 received :- 137ᴬ Field Ambulance with Headquarters at HEUDICOURT and with detachment at NURLU will continue to collect sick and wounded from Rifle Brigade, Sir at SOREL-LE-GRAND to be collected by 136ᴬ Field Ambulance, which will take over Divisional Main Dressing Station (former C.A.D.S.) at V 18 c on July 10. Taken on strength.	
		4	CAPT. A.H. LITTLE, R.A.M.C. reported for duty from LE TREPORT.- Taken on strength.	
		7	23 O.R's R.A.M.C. reported from Base Details :- taken on strength	
	11		1 O.R. R.A.M.C. transferred to No 350 Sanitary Section and struck off strength	see App. 2
	12		Reconstitution of battalions in the line - R.A.P's and Bearer Post's changed	
	13	A.M. 9	Memo received from O.C. A.D.S. asking permission to dig a dug-out at A.D.S. owing to numerous frequency of enemy shelling and scanty protection offered by present cellars and cupolas. A.D.M.S. 40ᵗʰ Division writes in on this subject - A.D.M.S. agrees to 0.1' unsuitability of present site and pens instructions for O.C. Fd. Amb. to select a suitable site in cellars a similar nature.	
		Noon 12		
		P.M. 2	Visited VILLERS-GUISLAIN, inspected various cellars and found suitable accommodation (absent occupied) at X 9 a 2.2. Telephoned to A.D.M.S. to secure this site	

WAR DIARY or INTELLIGENCE SUMMARY

Army Form C. 2118.

Volume XIV
July 1917
137th Field Ambulance, R.A.M.C.

Place	Date	Hour	Summary of Events and Information	Remarks and references to Appendices
HEUDICOURT	14		Negotiations proceeding with A.D.M.S., C.R.E. and 121 Bde. for handing over and taking over of the cellars as A.D.S.	
			CAPT. J.O'S. BEVERIDGE, R.A.M.C. attached for temporary duty as M.O.I/c 21 Pickets in relief of CAPT. C. O'MALLEY, R.A.M.C. who was attached to this unit for 21 days.	
	15	P.M. 12.30	Telephone message received at NURLU by O.C. Fd. Amb. (who was inspecting the Dressing Stations) from O.C. A.D.S. VILLERS GUISLAIN to the effect that the A.D.S. was destroyed by shell fire and that he was moving to another site. Orders recalled the officer to NURLU to D.C. G.A.2.2 notified.	
			Notified A.D.M.S.	
		2	Visited VILLERS GUISLAIN and found cellars at D.C.G.A.2.2. still occupied by N.Z.E. Coppers officers. R.E. and Lieut. Col. A.D.M.S. received orders from him to move to D'ors. Divn. Ambulance which was very heavy and lasted 20 minutes (from 9 a.m. to 9.30 a.m.) - at 11.46. of 12 Ills. the ranks (3:9 and 4:2) - 2 officers and 2 O.R's slightly wounded and remained at duty. Kitchen and one cupola destroyed. Only fatal was to one O.R. with two ad. to was.	
			moved to cellars adjacent.	
		7	A.D.S. reopened at cellars at D.C.G.A.2.2. RMO's 21.Rd.H.H.N. O.C Field Amb. notified.	See App. 3
	16	A.M. 11.30	121 Inf. Bde. Orders No. 113 Copy No. 11 received - Relief of Bde. in the line & change of location of Hd.Qrs.	

Army Form C. 2118.

WAR DIARY
or
INTELLIGENCE SUMMARY

(Erase heading not required.)

137th Field Ambulance, R.A.M.C.

Volume XIV July 1917

Place	Date	Hour	Summary of Events and Information	Remarks and references to Appendices
HEUDICOURT	16		1 O.R. R.A.M.C. evacuated sick to 1' C.C.S.	
	17		CAPT. P.M. EDWARDS, R.A.M.C. posted to 'Home Establishment' and struck off strength	
	20		1 N.C.O. posted to unit from 135th Fd. Amb.	
	26	AM 11	S.A.M.S. 3rd Corps visited Advanced Dressing Station and 1st Gp. of Field Ambulance	
	27		1 O.R. R.A.M.C. transferred to 1' 136th Fd. Amb. and struck off strength	
	29		LIEUT. G.J. FARIE R.A.M.C. reported his arrival from No. 10 Stationary Hospital - taken on the strength and detailed for temporary duty with 49th Division	
	30		1 O.R. R.A.M.C. reported his arrival for duty from 138th Fd. Amb. - taken on the strength	
	31		During the month the following number of patients have passed through the Field Ambulance: — 325 Other Ranks admitted to Fd. Amb. - all sick. Two officers and 11 O.R's. passed less sick to sister C.C.S. 9 Divisional train Nursing for admission - all sick. Six officers and 142 O.R's (including 33 Shell [gas cases]) sent for admission to 'CCS or A.D.S. - all wounded. Five officers and 184 O.R's (sick) obtained for a period not exceeding 48 hours and then sent for admission to A.D.S. (all sick) 164th O.R's. Sick and 9 O.R's. slightly wounded-treated and returned to duty. During the month the following battle casualties occurred in the Fd. Amb. — 2 officers, 2 O.R's. slightly wounded (sick) and on duty. 2 O.R's. passed and admitted to 40th C.C.S.	

[signature] LIEUT. COLONEL,
COMMANDING 1ST FIELD AMB.

Appendix I

SECRET.

Scheme of Evacuation from Right Brigade

Place	Map Reading	Personnel	Accommodation
H.Q. & Dr. Station	57c - W.21.b.3.9	—	50 patients
A.D.S.	X.9.c.0.7	2 Officers & 12 O.Rs	20 do
R.A.P. Left Bttn	X.2.b.8.2	4 bearers & One wheeled stretcher at each R.A.P.	—
Left Centre	X.2.b.9.0		—
Right do	X.3.d.6.3 (Temporary)		—
Right Bttn	X.15.b.8.2		—

Cases are brought by hand or wheeled stretcher from the four R.A.Ps to A.D.S at X.9.C.0.7.

The accommodation of this A.D.S is made up as follows:-

1 Cellar
6 Cupolas

8 cases

1. Medical Officer. 2. Med. Inspection Room.
3. 6 cases. 4. 6 cases.
5 & 6 not yet completed.

During the day serious cases are brought on wheeled stretchers to Car rendezvous situated at X.13.c.2.0 – a distance of about 2,000 yds; walking cases proceed on foot & are conducted to this point, thence cases are removed by Ambulance Cars to Hd Qrs, HEUDECOURT (W.21.b.3.9), or III C.M.D.S, FINS.

During the night Cars run into the village & evacuate cases direct from the A.D.S at X.9.c.0.7.

Cases on arrival at Hd Qrs of Field Ambulance at HEUDECOURT, are dealt with as follows:-

(a) Sick cases that are likely to recover quickly are detained here & treated.

(b) Other cases are sent to the III C.M.D.S

Appendix I
(Contd)

FINS by Horsed Ambulance or Car.

The Decauville Railway from REVELON to FINS is used daily at 11.30 a.m to clear sick cases to III C.M.D.S.

Seriously wounded cases are evacuated direct to C.C.S YTRES.

The morning sick etc from HEUDECOURT and VAUCELETTE FARM are seen at Hd Qrs Field Ambulance and cases requiring attention + rest are detained.

DECAUVILLE

Within a short time the Decauville Railway will be extended to VILLERS GUISLAINS. It will then be possible to evacuate wounded direct to III C.M.D.S from the A.D.S at X.9.c.0.7.

LIEUT. COLONEL,
R.A.M.C.
COMMANDING 187 FIELD AMBULANCE

Appendix. 2.

Alterations in the Position of the R.A.P's

Owing to the fact that instead of Four Battalions being in the line, only two were to be actually in the line, with one Battalion in Reserve and one in Support, the R.A.P's were altered as follows:-

New. R.A.P's.	Map Reading.	Remarks.
Left Battn in Line	X.3.b.9.0.	These alterations took place on 12/7/17.
Right do do	X.15.b.8.2.	
Battn in Support	X.3.d.25.15	
" Reserve.	X.13.c.7.0.	

Appendix 3.

The New Advanced Dressing Station.

Owing to the partial destruction of the A.D.S at X.9.c.0.7 on 15/7/17, it was necessary to find a new site. This was finally decided upon at X.9.a.2.2. The new A.D.S is situated in the large courtyard of a farm. In the same yard is a Water point — the well being worked by a Petrol Engine — and a Post of the Brigade Signals. A large cellar has been taken over and strutted by the R.E's, and stretcher racks placed to accommodate 40 lying cases. These alterations were completed 20/7/17.

Day & night working parties R.A.M.C have been employed, strengthening the roof with bricks and logs.

Two Cupolas were fetched from the old

Appendix 3
(Cont'd)

A.D.S. at X.9.c.07, and re-erected in the old stable in the courtyard. These Cupolas have been sandbagged and are now used to accommodate the Personnel. The two Medical Officers have been accommodated in a small cellar in the courtyard.

During the night the Motor Ambulance Cars proceed to this A.D.S. and are able to stand in the yard. There is a good road from the entrance to the yard to the main VILLERS GUISLAINS Road.

Method of Evacuation.

a. By Day.

During the daytime, walking cases proceed across country to VAUCELETTE FARM. Directing posts have been erected between the A.D.S. (at X.9.a.2.2) and VAUCELETTE FARM. Lying cases are brought by road on wheeled stretchers to the farm. All cases are then brought by Ambulance Cars from the Car Rendezvous at VAUCELETTE FARM either to Hd Qrs or taken direct to the 40 D.M.D.S. (The D.M.D.S. replaced the III.C.M.D.S. on 10/17).

The Decauville is still used to evacuate Sick cases in the Morning from REVELON to FINS. (40 Divisional Main Dressing Station.)

b. By Night

The Motor Ambulance Cars proceeds direct to the A.D.S. and cases are evacuated direct to C.C.S. or D.M.D.S. or brought to

Appendix 3
Concld.

the Hd Qrs of the Field Ambulance for treatment.

In time the Decauville Railway will go right up to the A.D.S — thus cases will then be sent direct to the D.M.D.S. if necessary.

At daybreak the Motor Ambulance bars leave the A.D.S and return to VAUCELETTE FARM for duty during the day.

R.A.M.C.
Commanding 187 Field Ambulance

14 d/2864

No. 137. F.O.

Aug. 1917

COMMITTEE FOR THE
MEDICAL HISTORY OF THE WAR
Date -1 OCT. 1917

Army Form C. 2118.

WAR DIARY
or
INTELLIGENCE SUMMARY.
(Erase heading not required.)

SECRET
Instructions regarding War Diaries and Intelligence Summaries are contained in F.S. Regs., Part II. and the Staff Manual respectively. Title pages will be prepared in manuscript.

Volume 15.

137th Field Ambulance R.A.M.C.

August 1917

Place	Date	Hour	Summary of Events and Information	Remarks and references to Appendices
HEUDICOURT (Sheet 57 C 1/40,000 W.21.b.39)	1	A.M. 11.30	1 Officer 23 O.R's returned from duty at Neuvy Station NURLU. All patients had been with transferred to 40th & Stat. Neuvy Station - discharged to "Billets" and the Neuvy Station closed. 2 Loading parties of 1 N.C.O. & 2 Nco. Left to guard buildings etc. until lease of same handed over to Town Major.	
		P.M. 3	121st Inf. Bde Operation Order No 116 Ltr App A·8 received - stating relief of right Battalion by a Battalion of 35nd Division on night 1st/2nd August. - Northern boundary of Brigade (and also of Division) will be: - DC 12 a 38, DC 11 a 0.0.6, X 10 b 3.7, X 10 a 2.0, X 5 b 2.8, X 20 a 9.8, X 19 c 74, DC 23 a 1.6, joining existing boundary at DC 30 c 0.4. On night 2/3 August, a Battalion 121st Inf. Bde will relieve a Battalion of 119th Inf. Bde in GRUNCHEZ Wood. - Northern Boundary of Brigade will be: - R 22 c 0.0, R 27 a 9.4, EIN AVENUE GREEN SWITCH at junction of trench R 31 d 8.5'15, reference to 119th Inf. Bde Trace L.'Trier H 16 d 6.3'0.3, joining present boundary at W 12 t 0.3.	
		9	Copy of new boundary of 121st Inf. Bde sent to O.C. Advanced Dressing Stn. VILLERS BURCAIN, Order on above received from O.C. 2nd Arg, to O.C. A.D.S. VILLERS BURCAIN instructs R.A.M.C. personnel from Bearer Post, Right Battalion, Right Brigade. (MANANCOURT) & 131 F.R.8.2.	
	2	A.M. 10.30	Addressed to 1st & 121st Inf. Bde Operation Order No 116 Copy No 8 received - having suffered & rosave Env.	

T2134. Wt. W708-776. 500000. 4/15. Sir J. C. & S.

Army Form C. 2118.

WAR DIARY
or
INTELLIGENCE SUMMARY

137th Field Ambulance, R.A.M.C.
Volume 15. August 1917.

(Erase heading not required.)

Place	Date	Hour	Summary of Events and Information	Remarks and references to Appendices
HEUDICOURT	2	AM. 11	Orders sent to O.C. A.D.S. Villers Guislain to arrange for evacuation of sick and wounded from 137/1 Battalion in Gonnelieu Sector.	See Appendix I
		PM. 1	40th Division R.A.M.C. Operation Order No. 31 copy No. 11 received — giving new orders and Southern Divisional boundaries. 133rd Field Ambulance (flows sufficient) removed from 137th Field Ambulance) will clear casualties from the front line. Say 120th, 119th and 119th and 119th and 121st Battalion. O. Tp. 121st Inf. Bde. L.M.G. advanced Dressing Station at P. 29 d. 2. 9. 133rd Field Ambulance (less personnel attached to 133rd Field Ambulance) will clear to front line Field Dy 121st Inf. Bde. Plus M.T. Lorry to 121st Battalion. M. advanced Dressing Station at D.C. 9. a. 2.2. Details to be arranged by O.C. unit.	
		2	Proceeded to M.A. 133rd Fd. Amb. C.V. Interview O.C. that unit — then officer in to inform 137th Fd. Amb. the number & details personnel arrangement made for him to inform 137th Fd. Amb. the number & details personnel to replace.	Addendum I to App. I
		3.5	Amendment to orders of today; date; nov. 2 to O.C. A.D.S. Villers Guislain.	
	3	AM. 9	Communication received from O.C. 133rd Fd. Amb. that the date of regnd. army personnel from 137th Amb.	
		PM. 3.30	The Quartermaster and 1 Staff Sergt. attached letters at SOREL on Catering by D/Q of Catering 3rd Army.	

SECRET

Army Form C. 2118.

WAR DIARY
or
INTELLIGENCE SUMMARY

(Erase heading not required.)

Volume 15. 137th Field Ambulance R.A.M.C.
August 1917

Place	Date	Hour	Summary of Events and Information	Remarks and references to Appendices
HEUDICOURT	4	Noon 12	1 Corporal Cook despatched to '3rd Army School of Cookery' for 3 weeks Course.	
	5		CAPT. C. O'MALLEY, R.A.M.C. returned to 21st Field Amb. for duty. — CAPT. J.O.S. BEVERIDGE, R.A.M.C. returned to this Field Ambulance from 21st Amb. A/N	
		P.M. 7	2 N.C.O's sent to '40th Divisional Gas School' for 3 days course of instruction	
	7	A.M. 11	CAPT. A.H. LITTLE R.A.M.C. att' to '3rd Bn Yorks R.gt.' for temporary duty in relief of CAPT. W. BROWNLIE R.A.M.C. proceeding on leave.	
	8	A.M. 9	22 O.R's R.A.M.C. despatched for temporary duty with 138th Field Ambulance, FINS	
		Noon 12	6 Riding horses inspected by Deputy Director of Remounts at Divisional Headquarters. These horses to be eventually withdrawn from the Field Ambulance - war establishment to be restricted to a Pair of 2 - 8 Riding horses instead of 14.	
	9	P.M. 3	Pay Box Refunds Field Cashier opened - each officer N.C.O and man in the undercicled Horse & Harness continues drill weekly in small box respirators	
	10	A.M. 9.30	Interviewed O.C. No 10 Canadian Fd. Amb. Cy re relief by and or O.C. No 6 Canadian Fd. Amb. Cy Entrainment at FINS. Also arranged by wksly Accommodation Cty from pres-line Hd. Gs. of G.A.S. to VILLERS GUISLAIN - terminus of Decauville Rly. 28.8.90.30.	
	11		1 N.C.O. detailed as Gas N.C.O. at Advanced Dressing Station	

SECRET

Army Form C. 2118.

Instructions regarding War Diaries and Intelligence **Volume 15.**
Summaries are contained in F.S. Regs., Part II.
and the Staff Manual respectively. Title pages **August 1917**
will be prepared in manuscript.

WAR DIARY
or
INTELLIGENCE SUMMARY
(Erase heading not required.)

137th Field Ambulance R.A.M.C.

Place	Date	Hour	Summary of Events and Information	Remarks and references to Appendices
HEUDICOURT	13	A.M. 9	CAPT A.J. BEVERIDGE R.A.M.C. commenced a 3 days course at 40th Div. Gas School, FINS.	
	15		1 O.R. R.A.M.C. arrived from Cyclist-Base Depot - taken on strength.	
	16		1 O.R. R.A.M.C. evacuated sick to C.C.S.	
	20		1 O.R. R.A.M.C. posted from 135th Fd. Amb. and taken on strength.	
	21	A.M. 8.30	CAPT J.M. LINNELL R.A.M.C. detached to temporary duty with 38th Heavy Artillery Group. Visited A.D.M.S. and received verbal orders to take over to 40th Divisional Main Dressing Station - relief to be completed by 6 P.M. 23rd inst. Arrangements to be made whilst acting O.C. 136th Fd. Amb.	
		P.M. 2	CAPT A.J. BEVERIDGE, LIEUT and QMr J. REID and one Corpls[?] return to 137th Field Ambulance and 1 O.R. "D" D.M.D.S. (V.18.c) as advance party.	
		4.40	40th Division of Order (R.A.M.C.) No. 32 Copy No 12 received stating :- 137th Field Ambulance will take over with Advanced Dressing Station at HEUDICOURT and KILLER GUISCAIN will take over charge of the Divisional Main Dressing Station at V.18.c. from 136th Field Ambulance. Taking over and handing over to be completed by 6 P.M. on the 23rd inst.	
		9	Message received from O.C. Section at V.18.c. that 136th Fd. Amb. was to move out from D.M.D.S. V.18.c. at 10 a.m. 22-8-17. Arrangements made to move 1st Pt. of unit	

A6945 Wt. W14422/M1160 350,000 12/16 D.D. & L. Forms/C./2118/14.

Army Form C. 2118.

WAR DIARY
or
INTELLIGENCE SUMMARY.
(Erase heading not required.)

SECRET.

Volume 'B' 137th Field Ambulance R.A.M.C.

August 1917

Place	Date	Hour	Summary of Events and Information	Remarks and references to Appendices
HEUDICOURT	21		137 HEUDICOURT to EINS (V.18.c.) at 10.30 A.M. 22-8-1917 and on 10th area charge of A.D.M.S. from 10 A.M. 22 inst.	
EINS (V.18.c.)	22	A.M. 11.30	2nd Field Ambulance less 1 Section at V.18.c. and detachment at A.D.S. VILLERS GUISLAIN	
		P.M. 4	Col. HEUDICOURT arrived w/ D.M.D.S. V.18.c.	
			CAPT. A.H. LITTLE, R.A.M.C. returned from temporary duty with 13th Yorkshire R/t.	
	23	A.M. 9	3 O.Rs. R.A.M.C. dispatched as Nurses Attendants and to joint 2" D.A.M.C. ST. OMER.	
			22 O.Rs. R.A.M.C. returned from temporary duty with 135th Fd. Amb.	
		P.M. 2	CAPT. A.J. BEVERIDGE R.A.M.C. detailed for temporary duty as M.O. i/c 20th Middlesex. R.f.	
			1 O.R. R.A.M.C. evacuated sick to C.C.S.	
	25		1 O.R. R.A.M.C. dispatched to corps of Corbey or 3rd Army School of Cookery ALBERT.	
		A.M. 10.30	LIEUT. C.J. BUCKLEY R.A.M.C. dispatched to 19th R. held bn. for temporary duty as M.O.	
		P.M. 6	CAPT. A.J. BEVERIDGE R.A.M.C. returned from temporary duty with 20th Middlesex R/t.	
	26	P.M. 4	CAPT. B.B. NESTLAKE R.A.M.C. arrived for temporary duty from 135th Fd. Amb.	
			1 N.C.O. R.A.M.C. returned from 3 weeks course of cookery at 3rd Army School of Cookery ALBERT.	
	27		O.Rs. R.A.M.C. taken on the strength from 135th Fd. Amb.	
	29		LIEUT. C.F. LAVER, U.S.M.C. reported arrival and taken on the strength.	

SECRET

Army Form C. 2118.

WAR DIARY
or
INTELLIGENCE SUMMARY.
(Erase heading not required.)

137th Field Ambulance, R.A.M.C.
August 1917 Volume XV

Place	Date	Hour	Summary of Events and Information	Remarks and references to Appendices
FINS (V.18.c)	30		LIEUT. G.J. EARIE, R.A.M.C. posted to 136th H. Amb. and struck off strength.	
	31		CAPT. M.W. ROBERTSON, R.A.M.C. attached for temporary duty from 136th Fd. Amb. During the month the following casualties have passed through the Field Ambulance:— Officers:— Wounded 7; O.Rs:— Wounded 40, Sick 323. Other Ranks:— Wounded 1 (29-8-17) Other Ranks:— Wounded 9 – Officers Sick 1 – O.R's Sick 1063 – have been treated and returned to duty without their units.	

R.W.Webb
LIEUT. COLONEL,
R.A.M.C.
COMMANDING 137 FIELD AMBULANCE

APPENDIX TO AUGUST DIARY.

APPENDIX. I.   SECRET.

O.C.
A.D.S. VILLERS GUISLAIN

Please arrange the following distribution of R.A.M.C. Bearer Posts night of 2nd/3rd August:-

1 Squad with 12th Suffolks Regt. — H.Q. R.26.d.7.7.
1 Squad " 20th Mdx. Regt — H.Q. X.3.d.7.3.
1 Squad " 13th Yorks Regt — H.Q. X.2.b.7.1.

If accommodation can be obtained, you should place a Relay Bearer Post at KITCHIN CRATER, (R.33.c.8.8).

The Evacuation of cases from all the R.A.P.s of the Brigade (less the 21st Middlesex R.A.P) will be through A.D.S. VILLERS GUISLAIN.

Render a report on the Reserve Bearer Post & its suitability. If you can find a better site, please inform me.

(sgd) N. E. Dunkerton,
LIEUT. COLONEL,
R.A.M.C.
COMMANDING 137 FIELD AMBULANCE

AMENDMENT TO APP: I.   SECRET.

O.C. A.D.S. VILLERS GUISLAIN.

Reference my X/97 of to-day's date.

Cancel "One Squad with 12 Suffolk Regt - H.Q. R.26.d.7.7."

Cancel "If accommodation can be obtained, you should place a Relay Bearer Post at KITCHIN CRATER (R.33.c.8.8)."

Cancel last two paragraphs.

Extract from 40 Division R.A.M.C. O. Order N° 31.

"As far as the 121st Bde is concerned you will clear casualties from Right Battn & Support Battn + any details in village."

(sgd) N. E. Dunkerton
LIEUT. COLONEL,
R.A.M.C.
COMMANDING 137 FIELD AMBULANCE

140/2438

No. 137. 7.a.

Sept. 1917

COMMITTEE FOR THE
MEDICAL HISTORY OF THE WAR
Date -5 NOV. 1917

SECRET

Army Form C. 2118.

WAR DIARY
or
INTELLIGENCE SUMMARY
(Erase heading not required.)

Volume 16   September 1917

137th Field Ambulance, R.A.M.C.

Place	Date	Hour	Summary of Events and Information	Remarks and references to Appendices
FINS (Sheet 57C) V 18 c.	3	AM 10.30	CAPT. R.B. HESTLAKE, R.A.M.C. returned to 'duty' with 135nd Field Ambulance. D.D.M.S. IIIrd Corps inspected Divisional Main Dressing Station.	
	4			
	7	P.M. 4	CAPT. J.W. LINNELL, R.A.M.C. returned from temporary duty with 21st Heavy Artillery Group. 10 P.B. Batmen (Infantry) arrived from No. 2 P.B. Base — taken on the strength. 10 O.R's A.S.C. (H.T.) despatched to "I" A.S.C. H.T. Depot, Base.	
	8	A.M. 8	6 Surplus Riders to I'2' A.D.R. IIIrd Army	
	9		LIEUT. C.J. BUCKLEY, U.S.R. returned from temporary duty with 19th Royal Welsh Fusiliers.	
	10	NOON 12	CAPT. P.G. FOULKES, R.A.M.C. despatched for temporary duty with 13th R. Welsh Regt.	
		P.M. 6.30	Consulting Surgeon, Third Army visited D.M.D.S. and lectured on "Crural Surgery"	
	11		CAPT. J.O.S. BEVERIDGE, R.A.M.C. detached for temporary duty with 189th Bde. R.F.A.	
	13	NOON 12	D.M.S. Third Army inspected D.M.D.S.	
		P.M. 3.15	D.M.S. Third Army inspected A.D.S. at VILLERS GUISLAIN	
	16		1st LIEUT. L.M. SANKEY, U.S.R. arrived to 'duty' and taken on the strength.	
		P.M. 6	CAPT. P.G. FOULKES, R.A.M.C. returned from temporary duty with 13th Bn. Yorkshire Regt. Non Officer Commission (Medical) visited D.M.D.S.	
	17		CAPT. A.H. LITTLE, R.A.M.C. posted as M.O. to 11th Bn. K.O. Royal Lancashire Regt. & struck off strength	

Army Form C. 2118.

WAR DIARY
or
INTELLIGENCE SUMMARY.
(Erase heading not required.)

137th Field Ambulance R.A.M.C.
Volume 16
September 1917

Place	Date	Hour	Summary of Events and Information	Remarks and references to Appendices
FINS	19		CAPT. J. O. S. BEVERIDGE R.A.M.C. returned from temporary duty with 181st Bde. R.F.A.	
	23		CAPT. J. O. S. BEVERIDGE R.A.M.C. temporary detail as M.O. to 12th S.W.B.	App. I
	25	P.M. 7.30	Raid by 12th Buffers Regt. on Wooden Trenches R.28 (sheet 57C ---)	
	27	P.M. 6	DDMS III Corps inspected D.H.Q.S.	
	30	P.M. 8.30	CAPT. M. W. ROBERTSON R.A.M.C. 136th Field Ambulance Takes 137th Field Ambulance Hospital for England on transfer of establishment.	
			Burnt to maint[ain] to others casualties and admitted to Fd. Ambs. —	
			Officers. Sept 31. Wounded 15 (include 1 Russian of May)	
			O.R's — G.S. 848. Wounded 228 (include 3 Russian of May)	
			Sick Total ... ... Officers 14 O.R's 1034	
			Sick Total and returned to duty ... ... O.R's 3.	
			Hospital	
			On September 26th Two N.C.O's sent on fronts of 75 Field Ambulance were awarded the Military Medal for an act of bravery performed on September 20th, 1917	

[signature]
LIEUT. COLONEL,
R.A.M.C.
COMMANDING 137 FIELD AMBULANCE

Reference:- Sheet. 57C SE 1/20,000

System of Evacuation of Casualties night of 25/26th Sept 17

	Medical Officers	N.C.Os	Ptes	Cars	Remarks
Relay Post - Poppy Post (X.2.d.9.9)	1	1(a)	3		(a) 1 Cpl (MT)
R.A.P. (Cheshire Quarry) (R.34.c.3.9)			8		R.A.M.C Stretcher bearers with wheeled stretchers
Relay Post Kitchen Crater (R.33.c.8.8)		1	6		
A.D.S. Villers Guislain (X.9.a.2.2)	2	3(b)	19	6(c)	(b) Includes 1 Sergt (MT) (c) Includes One large car + one Ford car working to the A.D.S, & the rest between A.D.S & Railton.
A.D.S. Heudecourt (W.21.b.3.9)	1				In reserve.
Railton		1	9(d)		(d) 8 Ptes R.A.M.C to load the Ambulance Trucks. One Pte to provide hot cocoa for patients.
Vaucellette Farm			2 (Nomad Amb co)		To evacuate sitting cases from Vaucelette Farm to D.M.D.S
Railton					Decauville Ambulance Trains to evacuate cases direct to C.C.S

All personnel were in their respective positions before zero time. The N.C.O & 14 Ptes at the R.A.P & Relay Post Kitchen Crater had been attached to the M.O i/c 12th Suffolks the previous night & had been taken over the proposed routes by that Officer in order that they would be familiar with the tracks.

Between 8.30pm & 3.30 A.M cases were removed by Wheeled Stretchers from the R.A.P to the Relay Post at Kitchen Crater, but from 1.0 am onwards the evacuations were very intermittent as Patrol parties from the Battalion had to be sent out to find the wounded. It can easily be seen that this caused the evacuations to be spasmodic, but no delay was experienced in evacuating cases from one post to another.

From KITCHEN CRATER cases were removed to POPPY POST by Wheeled Stretchers up to 1.0am, but from that time onwards, a Ford Car ran between the former post and the A.D.S (V.G), although the Wheeled Stretchers were still used between the CRATER & POPPY POST.

Up to 1.0am evacuations from POPPY POST to the A.D.S (V.G) were carried out by the Ford Car & the large Ambulance Car, but after that time, the Ford Car, as stated above, was diverted to run between KITCHEN CRATER & the A.D.S (V.G) while the large Car continued to clear cases from POPPY POST.

In consequence of this arrangement, it was only necessary to send one small batch of walking cases through the village of VILLERS GUISLAIN.

Four large Ambulance Cars were stationed at the A.D.S. (V.G) to evacuate all cases to the Decauville Ambulance trains at RAILTON (W.16.d). At first, it was intended to bring the Ambulance Trains up to the A.D.S (V.G) & load there, but unfortunately the enemy had been shelling in the afternoon & it was found that the Decauville Line was severely damaged for a distance of 150 yards, approximately near X.13.b to X.7.d.

The cases on arrival at RAILTON were loaded on the Ambulance Trains. Hot cocoa was supplied to all patients at RAILTON, a R.A.M.C Pte having been detailed for this duty.

The cases were evacuated to C.C.S from RAILTON by Ambulance Trains as follows:-

Train	Cases		Times	
	Stretcher	Sitting	Dep. Railton	Arr. Ypres
1st Train	12	4	1.25 am	3.20 am
2nd Train	8	-	3.45 am	5.50 am
3rd Train	15	-	6.15 am	7.40 am
Totals	35	4	-	-

In all 35 stretcher cases & 4 sitting cases were evacuated by the Decauville Ambulance Trains. A new Ambulance Truck was used & proved a success. It is understood that the length of time taken by the trains in the journeys was due to the breaking down of the telephone arrangements on the Decauville & also to the heavy fog.

One Pte R.A.M.C was detailed to accompany each Ambulance Truck from RAILTON to YPRES.

24 Walking cases were sent from A.D.S (V.G) to the Bar Head VAUCELETTE FARM (X.13.a.c.7) where the two Horsed Ambulance Wagons were stationed, which then conveyed these cases to the 40th D.M.D.S. (V.18.c).

The remaining cases (4 Officers 7. O.Rs) were brought direct to the D.M.D.S. by the Ambulance Cars on their return from the A.D.S (V.G).

One wounded German Prisoner was evacuated lying to the C.C.S. by Decauville.

LIEUT. COLONEL,
R.A.M.C.
COMMANDING 137 FIELD AMBULANCE

140/2499

No. 137 7 O

COMMITTEE FOR THE
MEDICAL HISTORY OF THE WAR
Date -8 DEC. 1917

WAR DIARY or INTELLIGENCE SUMMARY

Army Form C. 2118.

137th Field Ambulance. R.A.M.C.

October 1917 Volume 17

Place	Date	Hour	Summary of Events and Information	Remarks and references to Appendices
FINS (Sheet 57C 1/40,000 V18c)	2	P.M. 4.30	40th Division R.A.M.C. Order No. 33 copy No. 12 received. — The 40th Division will be relieved by the 20th Division between the 6th and 11th of October, and will move into 7th Corps area and Division will be — 137th Field Ambulance to be completed by 3 P.M. 9th inst. Start of relief to be arranged direct between O's.C. concerned.	
				9/10/17
PERONNE	3	P.M. 4.25	Amendment to O.O. No. 33 received — All moves are advanced 24 hours.	
		8.20	Addendum to O.O. No. 33 received — The date of landing over 1st Field Ambulance of 20th Div 20th.	
	4	A.M. 10	Lieut. C.F. Lowes, U.S.R. temporarily attached to duty as M.O. 1/c 40th S.A.C.	
	5	P.M. 3.30	121st Inf. Bde. Operation Order No. 141 Copy No. 8 received. — On October 10, 137th Field Ambulance will move as follows:— By road SOREL to PERONNE. On October 11 and 12 to Brigade Group (includes 137th H. Amb.) will move by road and rail to 7th Corps Area (BARLY)	
		4	61st Field Ambulance, 20th Division arrived at D.A.D.S. and settled accommodation pending their taking over.	
	6	P.M. 8.15	Proceeded with O.C. 61st Field Ambulance to A.D.S. VILLERS GUISLAINS with a view to his becoming acquainted with the Sector.	
	7	P.M. 10	12 O.R's 61st H. Amb. and 1 Officer proceeded to A.D.S. VILLERS GUISLAINS and relieved the	

SECRET

Army Form C. 2118.

WAR DIARY
or
INTELLIGENCE SUMMARY

(Erase heading not required.)

Volume 17 137th Field Ambulance
October 1917

Place	Date	Hour	Summary of Events and Information	Remarks and references to Appendices
FINS (V18c)	7		Same number of personnel of 137th Fd. Amb. CAPT. J.W. LINNELL, R.A.M.C. still in command of A.D.S. and Bearer Posts.	
	8	Non 12	Handed over Baths at HEUDICOURT to Representatives of 20th Division. Personnel withdrawn.	
		P.M. 3	Handed over A.D.S. at HEUDICOURT to 61st Field Ambulance. Personnel of 137th Fd. Amb. withdrawn to FINS.	
		P.M. 10	Relief by 61st Fd. Amb. at Bearer Posts and A.D.S. VILLERS GUISLAIN completed. CAPT. J.W. LINNELL and remainder of 137th Fd. Amb. Personnel returned to Hd Qrs Fd. Amb. FINS.	
	9	Non 12	Handed over Baths at SOREL and NURLU to The respective Town Majors. Personnel withdrawn to Hd Qrs Fd. Amb.	
			Handed over Divisional Main Dressing Station (V18c) to 61st Field Ambulance. 20th Division 137th Field Ambulance remained in its present quarters till the next evt.	
	10	A.M. 8.30	Handed over Field Ambulance site at NURLU to Town Major NURLU This unit had been removed to a Field Ambulance — two O.R.'s 137th Fd. Amb. having been attached there since a return of Fd. Amb. vacated the buildings on August 1, 1917.	
		A.M. 9	Relief of D.D.M.S. handed over to 61st Fd. Amb. Field Ambulance completed. Proceeded by march route to PERONNE are NURLU, AIZECOURT-LE-HAUT.	

Army Form C. 2118.

WAR DIARY
or
INTELLIGENCE SUMMARY

(Erase heading not required.)

SECRET. Volume 17. 137th Field Ambulance R.A.M.C.
October 1917.

Place	Date	Hour	Summary of Events and Information	Remarks and references to Appendices
PERONNE Sheet 62.C 1/40,000 I.27.b.	10	12.45 PM	Unit arrived at PERONNE. Routed to JOCK STREET. Field Ambulance remained closed.	
		10.30 PM	Orders received from H.Q. 41st Inf. Bde. for Transport (less 2 Ambulances and two mules) to proceed by road route with Brigade Transport to BAPAUME area at:-	
		7.30 A.M. 11th inst.		
			Verbal order from Brigade HQrs. 121st Inf. Bde. that Unit less Transport would proceed by road	
			to the new area on the 12th inst.	
	11	7.30 AM	Horse Transport of unit, plus 2 Ambulance-wagons five mules and two spare mules under Capt. A.J. BEVERIDGE, R.A.M.C. proceeded by road route to BAPAUME area.	
	12	9 AM	Moto ambulance cars under Capt. J.W.LINNELL, R.A.M.C. proceeded by road to BARLY	
		1.30 PM	Field Ambulance (less Transport) entrained at FLAMICOURT, PERONNE, to new area	
		2 PM	Moto ambulance cars arrived at BARLY	
		5 PM	Horse Transport arrived at BARLY	
		6.45 PM	Field Ambulance detrained at BEAUMETZ-LES-LOGES	
BARLY Sheet 5/10 1/40,000 Pic d.2.7.		11.5 PM	Field Ambulance less Transport arrived at BARLY	
	13	12 Noon	Capt. P.G. FOULKES, R.A.M.C. proceeded to W.Wilkins to Company duty as M.O.	
	14	5 PM	Capt. J.O's BEVERIDGE, R.A.M.C. returned from Temporary duty with 12th Bn. "O Brokes"	

Army Form C. 2118.

WAR DIARY or INTELLIGENCE SUMMARY.

(Erase heading not required.)

137D Field Ambulance

Volume 17 October 1917

Place	Date	Hour	Summary of Events and Information	Remarks and references to Appendices
BARLY	21	A.M. 9	CAPT. A.J. BEVERIDGE, R.A.M.C. over medical charge of 40th Div. Rft Battalion SAULTY.	
	23	10.30	1st LIEUT. C.J. BUCKLEY, M.O. R.C. U.S.A proceeded for temporary duty as M.O. i/c R.E. 49th Division	
	25	P.M. 3	1st Lieut. C.T. LAVER, M.O. R.C. U.S.A returned from temporary duty as M.O. i/c R.A.C.	
	26	Noon 12	Morning Orders received from A.D.M.S. - Training will continue to the end of October 29 and 30 Training stations BEAUMETZ-LES-LOGES and SAULTY	
	27	A.M. 9.30	Orders received from H.Q. 121st Infantry Brigade to render without-delay "Training state".	
		P.M. 12.15	Reference warning order received from G.S.O.1 on 26th inst. further instructions received — Advance parties for each Brigade Group will RVTo MAROEUIL at 8.30 P.M. on 27th October 1917 to entrain for HAZEBROUCK.	
		P.M. 3	121st Infantry Brigade Order No. 143 Copy No 11 received — The Brigade Group will be prepared to move in a few hours by rail on 29th and 30th instant	
		5	Addendum No 1 to 121st Inf. Bde Order No 143 received — Advance parties to units will be held in readiness to proceed at 2 hours notice — 137 F.A Cont 1 O.R.	
		5.15	Orders received from A.D.M.S. cancelling warning order re Advance parties received at 12.15 P.M. As advance party will not proceed at present.	
		9	CAPT. P.G. FOULKES, R.A.M.C returned from temporary duty as M.O. i/c 21st Battalion M.G.N.	

Army Form C. 2118.

WAR DIARY
or
INTELLIGENCE SUMMARY

SECRET

137th Field Ambulance R.A.M.C.

October 1917 Volume 17

(Erase heading not required.)

Instructions regarding War Diaries and Intelligence Summaries are contained in F. S. Regs., Part II. and the Staff Manual respectively. Title pages will be prepared in manuscript.

Place	Date	Hour	Summary of Events and Information	Remarks and references to Appendices
BARLY	28	A.M. 11:30	121st Inf. Bde Order No 144 Copy No 8 received. — Warning Order. — 137th Fd Bde Order No 143 dated 27th October, 1917 is cancelled. The Brigade Group will now by march route to WARLUZEL on the 29th inst. 1 NCO 137th Fd Amb. to report to Bde Hd Qrs at 1 P.M. for orders.	
		P.M. 2:35	137th Division R.A.M.C. Order No 34 Copy No 12 received. — The Division (less Artillery) will be accompanied by one Divisional Supply Column, will march on the 29th October to the LUCHEUX area. 121st Bde Group from BARLY — BAVINCOURT area to SUS-ST-LEGER — WARLUZEL — SOMBRIN area BARLY and BAVINCOURT will be cleared by 9 A.M.	
		P.M. 6	121st Inf. Bde Order No 145 Copy No 9 received. — 137th Field Ambulance from BARLY to WARLUZEL via SOMBRIN. Starting point, Road junction P.14.B.3.0. Time 8.23 A.M. 29-10-1917. Rendezvous Transport to be clear of BARLY by 8.0 A.M.	
		9	Administrative Instruction attached with reference to 121st Brigade Order No 145 received. — A Field ambulance will be detailed by the O.C. 137th Fd. Amb. to march with each Battalion. These Ambulances will rejoin the 137th Fd. Amb. at WARLUZEL on completion of move. Instructions issued to from Brigade as to which of to 4 Battalions the 3 Field Ambulances and 5 wheeled stretchers allotted to. 12th Suffolks 13 Yorks and 29 Middlesex. The units were to set up Report states to [illegible]	

Army Form C. 2118.

WAR DIARY
or
INTELLIGENCE SUMMARY

(Erase heading not required.)

137th Field Ambulance

Volume 17
October 1917

Place	Date	Hour	Summary of Events and Information	Remarks and references to Appendices
BARLY	29	8	Field Ambulance (less Motor Transport whole left at 7.30 AM) moved off from billets.	
		8.25	Passed Starting Point and took up position in the column behind 121st T.M.B. and in front of 21st Field Amb. Coy.	
MARIEUX		9.25 PM	Field Ambulance arrived at new area and went into billets.	
(Sh. 51C O 10 c 10.5)		2.45	Warning Orders received from H.Q. 121st Inf. Bde. Total evacuation to be by B of Beaudricourt.	
			Field Ambulance would probably be moved to Beaudricourt.	
O 27 c 8.9			1 Officer and 1 NCO proceeded to BEAUDRICOURT to select billets	
		7.40 PM	Orders received from A.D.M.S. to embus Brigade Area with a view to taking over and working Baths in this area	
	30	9 AM	Proceeded to SOMBRIN & SUS-ST-LEGER and took Baths at Letter, Abuse Hospital The 6	
			A.D.M.S. at LUCHEUX at 11 AM	
		10 AM	Instructions received from 121st Bde. definitely cancelling move to BEAUDRICOURT.	
		5 PM	Orders received from A.D.M.S. to run Baths at SUS-ST-LEGER and SAULTY on 31st inst.	
	31	2 PM	Baths opened at SAULTY and SUS-ST-LEGER.	

N. M.
LIEUT COLONEL
R.A.M.C.
COMMANDING 137 FIELD AMBULANCE

COMMITTEE FOR THE
MEDICAL HISTORY OF THE WAR
Date 17 JAN. 1918

WAR DIARY or INTELLIGENCE SUMMARY

Army Form C. 2118.

137th Field Ambulance R.A.M.C.

November 1917 — Volume 18

Place	Date	Hour	Summary of Events and Information	Remarks and references to Appendices
WARLUZEL	1	P.M. 3	1st/Lieut. L.M. SANKEY, M.O. R.C. USA attached for temporary duty as M.O./c 3rd Corps Reinforcement Camp	
(Sheet 51C 1/40,000 O 27 & 28)	7	A.M. 10	1st/Lieut. C.F. LAUER, M.O. R.C. USA attached for temporary duty as M.O./c 12th Bn Reinforcement Camp	
	9	P.M. 3	1st/Lieut. L.M. SANKEY returned from 3rd Corps Reinforcement Camp	
	10	P.M. 6	1st/Lieut. C.J. BUCKLEY, M.O. R.C. USA Returned from temporary duty with H.Q. 40th Div R.E.	
	14	P.M. 12.45	Orders received from A.D.M.S. to close the BATHS at SUS-ST-LEGER and SAULTY w.e.f. 4 P.M.	
			Orders received from O.C. 40th Div to dump self sufficient Billets at 40th Div Training (MT)(M.T.) Bn.	
			SAULTY on 15th inst.	
		P.M. 6	40th Div. car into V'Plage on 15th inst.	
		P.M. 10.30	40th Div RAMC (Section Orders No. 35) Copy No. 12 received — The Brigades (Bn. Brigadier) TR. R.E.	
			2½ Fd. Coys R.E. and 12th Gordon (P.) will move from LUCHEUX Area to FOUFFLIN-Meer.	
	15	A.M. 8.20	November 16 Field Ambulance will be granted on the last move — 137 Fd Amb. will move from WARLUZEL	
			14th DH Fd. Ambn to 149 Coy. As 15' Reserved — Road Junction 0.17. B.6.3. Time 10.5 a.m. via	
			L'ARBRE on 16th inst. Starting point — Road Junction 0.17. B.6.3. Time 10.5 a.m. via	
			SOMBRIN. Column portion to proceed on 13th inst. and take over accommodation at the	
			16th inst. when left in BARLY	
	16	A.M. 10	Unit left WARLUZEL by road.	

WAR DIARY
or
INTELLIGENCE SUMMARY.

(Erase heading not required.)

Army Form C. 2118.

Volume 18   "137th" Field Ambulance

November 1917

Place	Date	Hour	Summary of Events and Information	Remarks and references to Appendices
BARLY	16	A.M. 11.33	Unit arrived and took over all billets.	
S/C 10.00	17	A.M. 2.40	131st Inf. Bde. Order No 130. Copy A.9 received. — The Brigade Group will move from FANEUX	
P.15.d.2.7			Bivouac to Cupola at ACHIET-LE-PETIT to the right of TC mile of 17/18 November 1917. Sector Ponte.	
			Bivouac Grids — ½ mile ANE of the Wood E. of LA HERRIERE 137 H Cook ½ Area Refs	
			d. 6.40 P.M. Issued Ambulance to necessary 3 of the Battalions of the Bole. of the Brigade	
			with Bus for Route orders	
		A.M. 7.30	14th Point L.M. SANKEY, U.S.M.R. proceeded to Advanced Dump W. to 48 C.C.S. YPRES	
		9 A.M.	3 O.R's. proceeded to Advanced tent subdivision by ACHIET-LE-PETIT	
		A.M. 11	Ambulances proceeded from 3rd Div. Rly. head destination of point 13 by Rly. head point	
			Mou. to S. to STA. West of ACHIET-LE-GRAND	
		P.M. 5.30	Units Q.H. BARLY to new area proceeding via BAVINCOURT, LA CAUCHIE, POMMIER	
			BIENVILLERS - AU - BOIS, HANNESCAMPS, BUCQUOY and ACHIET-LE-PETIT	
ACHIET-LE-GRAND	18	A.M. 12.30	Unit arrived in new area. Bivom ACHIET-LE-GRAND	
Shd. 37c 10.000		P.M. 7.45	121st Inf. Bde. Order No 131. Copy A. 7 received. — The Brigade front will now be partit. hand	
			from the ACHIET-LE-PETIT area to accommodation at ROCQUIGNY on the night 19/23th November 1917	
G.Q. d. 46.			Starting Point. — Road junction 200 yards S of T. of ACHIET-LE-GRAND STA. Time for 137th	

SECRET
Army Form C. 2118.

WAR DIARY
INTELLIGENCE SUMMARY

November 1917   137th Field Ambulance. R.A.M.C
Volume 18

Place	Date	Hour	Summary of Events and Information	Remarks and references to Appendices
ACHIET-LE-GRAND	18		Field Ambulance at Ass — 10.10 P.M. Ren'd — BIHUCOURT — BIEFVILLERS — BAPAUME — LE TRANSLOY	
	19	A.M. 9	3 O.R's proceeded as Billeting party to ROQUIGNY. Rear party of Brigade in ACHIET-LE-PETIT area and have been arranged as follows. Serious cases to No 45th and No 49 C.C.S. ACHIET-LE-GRAND — slight cases (Walking) within an hour) to 6th Casy. Regt. Station at BIHUCOURT.	
		P.M. 9.45	Unit. left camp for ROQUIGNY.	
ROQUIGNY Sheet 57C O 27 d 6.9 40,000	20	A.M. 2.50	Unit. arrived at Aibles in ROQUIGNY	
		9	Unit. placed under orders to move at ½ an hour's notice	
		P.M. 2.30	V Copy Medical arrangements received (Advance to 43 dated 19/11/17) Attended conference at Office A.D.M.S 40th Division R.A.M.C Quarters. Order to 37 Coys. No 13 — The 40th Division will now at once move to BEAUMETZ — DOIGNIES Area, and will the advance in an easterly direction. 137th Field Ambulance (less Motor Transport) supplemented by the Officers and Bearer Division and Horsed Ambulance Wagons of 136th Field Ambulance will follow 121st Infantry Brigade Officer Commanding 137th Field Ambulance will be responsible for all close control of Regl. water	

Army Form C. 2118.

WAR DIARY
or
INTELLIGENCE SUMMARY.
(Erase heading not required.)

137 Field Ambulance November 1917

Place	Date	Hour	Summary of Events and Information	Remarks and references to Appendices
ROCQUIGNY			All Regimental aid-posts, ADS with "Transport" will be posted this evening with 136th Field Ambulance at BARASTRE and offd. that time, They will come under orders of ADMS. dirl. Headquarters 137th Field Ambulance will move with 2nd Line Transport of 131st Fd. Amb. Casualties will be evacuated from the front line under existing arrangements. During the first phase all casualties will be sent to MDS of IV a Corps stated at BEVGNY and LERUGUIERE walking cases being directed down to CAMBRAI – BAPAUME Road to the MDS BEVGNY. On the advance Northwards Field Ambulances will make their own arrangements for both Advanced and Main Dressing Stations – Divisional being notified to ADMS as soon as possible.	
	20	6.30 P.M.	87 ORs, 3 Horsed Ambulance Wagons and 1 GS Limbered Wagon arrived from 136th Fd. Amb.	
		6 P.M.	3 Boys Ambulance Cars and 1 small amb Car detached for duty under ADMS	
	21	1.30 P.M.	Unit under orders 6/12/17 of R.A. Lt-Col ROCQUIGNY for BEAUMETZ-LES-CAMBRAI	
		4.0 P.M.	Arrived at BEAUMETZ-LES-CAMBRAI	
BEAUMETZ-LES-CAMBRAI	22		Orders received from DDMS 56 Div. See Appendix I	

Army Form C. 2118.

WAR DIARY
or
INTELLIGENCE SUMMARY.
(Erase heading not required.)

137 Field Ambulance

Instructions regarding War Diaries and Intelligence Summaries are contained in F.S. Regs., Part II. and the Staff Manual respectively. Title pages will be prepared in manuscript.

NOVEMBER 1917
Vol. XVIII

Place	Date	Hour	Summary of Events and Information	Remarks and references to Appendices
DEMICOURT	22	8/15 PM	Capt J.O.S. BEVERIDGE RAMC wounded on the by G GRAINCOURT	9/11/8
			Died at 11.40. Body to my H.C.C.S. Burial at LEBUCQUIERE	
	23	11 AM	Lieut C.F. LAUER M.O. USA turned for duty from 12th SUFFOLK Regt	
BERTINCOURT	24	12 PM	Unit marched to YTRES & entrained for BEAUMETZ LES LOGES	
BEAUMETZ LES LOGES	27	8 AM	Unit detrained & marched to BAILLEULMONT	
BAILLEULMONT	27	10.30 PM	Unit arrived at BAILLEULMONT & billeted in village	
	28	9 AM	Lieut C.F. LAUER MORC USA visits to MO of 2/10 MIDDLESEX Regt	
			Struck off strength	
		1.30 PM	Lieut R.M. EWBANKS, MORC USA & Lieut F.G. MAGUIRE MORC USA reported	
			arrival for duty & taken on strength	
	29	9.30 PM	Lieut R.M. EWBANKS temporary attached for duty at the 4th C.C.S.	
	30	6.0 PM	Warning order from DDMS Corps that these from ADMS 1st Division	
			was to be in support to move at "one's" hour	
			During the month Nos 22 + 2 + No 26 5 Canadian Sub Parks also unit	
			were 1 officer to 16 (Turkish), WV & NCO's wounded, 1 wounded	
			& at duty	

W. G. Carver M.M.C.
Capt RAMC
OC 137 Field Ambulance

A6945 Wt.W14422/M1160 350000 12/16 D. D. & L. Forms/C./2118/14.

Medical Arrangements in Forward Area during Operations of 40th Division, Period Nov. 22nd to Nov. 26th, 1917 inclusive.

22nd

11 a.m.
Information gleaned unofficially somewhere in the forenoon that the 119 Infantry Brigade & the 121 Infantry Brigade were likely to attack on the morrow, with the 120 Infantry Brigade in support.

Steps immediately taken to get into touch with Medical Officers of the 119 & 121 Infantry Brigades.

Bearer Divisions consisting of 2 Medical Officers & 88 o.Rs. with necessary medical equipment were detailed to be in readiness to move at once with Brigades.

2 p.m.
Bearer Officer received information from the 119 Infantry Bde that the Brigade would move off at 3-30 pm from Dorgnies.

3-15 p.m.
Without instructions from the A.D.M.S., Bearer Division 119 Infantry Bde moved off to join Brigade.

3-45 p.m.
Above joined Brigade west of Dorgnies, thence marching via Hermies to Graincourt, encountered great difficulty negotiating the swampy track through K.14 a.& b. and K.9 c & b., one horse ambulance wagon

being left stranded on the track.

10-30 p.m. Arrived Graincourt and immediately set out to find Dressing Station. Found Dressing Station belonging to Field Ambulance of 62 Division situated at E.30.c.3.0 still in occupation.

This being still working a search was made and another found at K5 B 5-4. This was cleaned up and opened for receiving cases.

Cases were received at about 12 midnight 22nd - 23rd. These were treated & detained.

Two cars wired for to A.D.M.S. to come to K.14.a.3.0.

23rd 4 A.M. By this time one N.C.O. + 8 bearers were attached to each Infantry Battn of the 119 Infantry Bde.

22nd 4 p.m. Reverting to the movements
① Of the Bearer division detailed to be attached to the 121 Infantry Bde. and
② The remainder of the personnel & equipment.

One N.C.O. + 8 bearers were attached to each Infantry Battn of the 121 Infantry Bde.

At the moment preparations were being made for the former to follow the Brigade, then on the move, the following orders were received from the ADMS.

Same operation order no 38 detailing Field Ambulance complete to march behind 119 Infantry Bde to Graincourt & establish an Advanced Dressing Station.

Route - Doignies, Hermies, Havrincourt.

As this arrived at Beaumetz some ¾ of an hour after the 119 Infantry Brigade were scheduled to leave Doignies, the Bearer Division, plus the rest of the Field Ambulance, faute de mieux followed the transport of the 101 Infantry Bde to which they had been attached by a previous order of the ADMS which had never been rescinded.

4-15 pm

This party moved off proceeding by march route via Doignies as far as the entrance to Demicourt. Here it was found that this route was impracticable.

Word was passed back from the infantry in front that the bridge over the canal on this road to Graincourt was impassable for transport larger than half a G.S. Limber wagon, so it was decided to turn round, & attempt to get to Graincourt via Hermies, & the route already described above as having been taken by the 119 Infantry Brigade.

On reaching the beginning of the swampy cross country track through K 14 A & B & K 9 c & b, it was found absolutely impossible for the Ambulance transport, so it was decided to park all the transport at Hermies with the exception of one GS limber wagon loaded with medical equipment, & move on with all the Bearer personnel to Graincourt.

In spite of heavy spare pairs of heavy draught horses being hitched on to this limber, it had to be abandoned about half way across the cross country track.

On reaching the main road somewhere about K 9 D 6-4, an attempt was made to reach Graincourt, but owing to the absence of guides, the intense darkness, & the exhaustion of the men, a return was made to Havrincourt where the personnel bivouaced for the night.

On the decision to proceed to Havrincourt, an officer was detailed to proceed to Graincourt via Havrincourt & the road through

K22, K16, K17, K11; to ascertain
the disposition of the 119 Infantry Bde.
Bearer Division.

23rd
4 a.m.
   This officer arrived at
Graincourt to find an Advanced
Dressing Station established at
K5 b5-4. capable of dealing
with the casualties of the Division.
   Immediately the personnel
were bivouacced at Havrincourt,
& Field Ambulance, accompanied
by the Sergt. Major, also proceeded
to Graincourt.

5-15 a.m.
   OC Field Ambulance,
accompanied by Sergt. Major, arrived
at ADS Graincourt.

   Shortly after his arrival
orders were sent to Officer in charge
details at Havrincourt to establish
relay bearer posts at K9 B6-9
and at K14 a 3.0. cases to
be carried from the A.D.S. Graincourt
to the first mentioned bearer post,
thence down the main Havrincourt
road to a point somewhere
about K9. D6.2, & thence by cross
country track to K14 a 3.0.

   At the same time a
wire was sent to the ADMS who was
in charge of the whole of the
motor transport of the three Field
Ambulances to ask for the cars to

6

be sent to K14 a 3.0, thence to proceed via Hermies to IV Corps Main Dressing Stations Beugny & Lebucquiere, the destinations named in RAMC HQ Divisional Operation Order No 39 dated 22/7.

These posts were established immediately Orders were received by Officer i/c of Details, but owing to the kindness of OC 108 Field Ambulance, 36 Division relay posts at K9 B6.9, where there was no cover, was changed almost immediately to the spare brick kilns used as an Advanced Dressing Station by his Ambulance at K9 b6-2, and the post at K14 a 3-0 was moved nearer Hermies to K19 b2-9 where there was another Advanced Dressing Station of the 36 Division Field Amb.

The full mode of evacuation being as follows as far as K19 B2-9
(1) From RAPs to ADS GRAINCOURT (K5-b5.4 by carry on wheeled-stretcher
(2) From ADS to Bearer Post (K9-b-6.2) by carry on wheeled stretcher
(3) From K9 b6.2 along the canal bank to bridge crossing at K15 a 2 b & thence to relay post at K14 a.6.2. by carry.
(4) From K14 a 6.2 again by carry to K19 b 2-9 where they were placed on motor Ambulances & taken to M.D.S of 108 Field Ambulance (36 Division)

4.

(c) From 108 Field Ambulance MDS to
CCS Ontin etc.

All parts save the ADS were common
to 137 Field Ambulance & 108 Field Ambulance
cases were carried in their turn by bearers
of either Ambulance & the same
procedure was adopted with care.

In view of the fact
however that no 40 Division cars
arrived until 4pm, evacuations
from this point were kindly
taken over by the Field Ambulance
of the 36 Division.

This line of evacuation
was ready for use by 9-30am 23/11.

10-30 am. The 40th Division assisted by
Tanks attacked Bourlon Wood &
Village. Casualties arrived immediately
and continued to be brought in
incessantly until midnight 25-26
when the Division was relieved.

On the night of the 23rd the
ADS became congested. It was obvious
that the number of bearers at the
disposal of the OC bearers was
inadequate & wires were sent
immediately to the ADMS for
extra assistance.

Owing to the almost
impassable condition of the ground,
the length of the carry, the total
inability to bring motor ambulance
cars into the village, and for
some time horse ambulances, the
exhaustion of the bearers owing

8

to the prolonged marching which preceeded the operations.

It is impossible for anyone who was not present to imagine the difficulties encountered.

23rd
1 p.m.

An alternative scheme of evacuation, utilised by the 2/3 West Riding Field Ambulance 62 Division, received from ADMS 40 Division directing that it should be adopted by the 134 Field Ambulance at once. This happened to be impossible at the time owing to pressure of casualties, & An Officer was sent to ADMS 40 Division to explain the situation, & a written description of the mode of evacuation in use was forwarded to ADMS 40 Division.

Owing to the non-arrival of reinforcements & cars, again demanded from the ADMS 40 Division by telegram. In the meantime the services of recently captured German prisoners were utilised for the purpose of carrying wounded.

6 p.m.

Every man available for bearing had arrived from 134 Field Ambulance details, left at Harmies.

10-30 p.m.

One officer, 24 ORs. & six light horse ambulances arrived from No 9 Cavalry Field Ambulance Metz, & assisted in the removal of wounded via the 51 Divisional Field Ambulance at Hesqueres.

11-30 pm	An officer was sent to G.O.C. 119 Infantry Bde to ask for assistance from the Brigade in the matter of bearers. This was not forthcoming so a telegram was sent to ADMS 40 Division asking for 500 bearers & 100 stretchers.
24th 7 a.m.	Somewhere about this time 3 officers & about 120 men of the 135 Field Ambulance arrived as reinforcement, after a forced march during the night from Beaulencourt. These were followed at about 8 A.M. by 2 officers & about 50 men of the 136 Field Ambulance, who had also marched through the night from Trescault.
10 A.M.	An officer of the 15th Motor Ambulance Convoy arrived at ADS Graincourt to acquaint us of the fact that he was able to bring cars to Flesquières & that if cases could be conveyed to the chateau in that village he would within 4 hours have 20 Motor Ambulance cars waiting there to clear them to Ypres. Later an urgent wire was received from ADMS 40 Division saying that under instructions from DDMS Fourth Corps all horse ambulance wagons available were to be used to convey cases to Flesquières where the 15th Motor Ambulance convoy was waiting to evacuate cases.

10

By this time 4 Horse Ambulance wagons of 135-6-7 Field Ambulances were in use at Graincourt & immediately commenced evacuating cases to barns at the north end of Flesquieres, the chateau being absolutely demolished.

One officer & 20 o.Rs. of the 135 Field Ambulance were detained at Flesquieres to act as a loading party, sentries being posted round the village to await & direct the Motor Ambulance convoy.

No Motor Ambulance Convoy arrived until 12 noon, 25th inst, in spite of repeated wires to ADMS & finally a direct wire to DDMS Fourth Corps was sent by OC 134 Field Ambulance at 8-15 AM 25/4, as a result of the report of the deplorable conditions existing at Flesquieres.

Before being evacuated some serious cases had been lying since 11:30 AM on the 24th inst until the arrival at 12 noon on the 25th of the M.A.C. All had to endure terrible sufferings in open barns in face of all conditions of weather.

25 inst.
8 AM

In view of the terrible state of affairs an additional officer & 20 men were sent to Flesquieres. Here fires were started & with the assistance of 3 YMCA helpers, with their equipment

11

tea urns, boilers etc, food & drink was given to 300 patients now awaiting evacuation.

11-30 AM. ADMS 40 Division arrived at Flesquieres & saw for himself the appalling state of affairs but would not accept any responsibility as all applications for Motor Ambulance Convoy had been forwarded by him.

12 noon. DDMS Fourth Corps arrived at Flesquieres & saw the existing conditions. With him was O/c MAC

The DDMS immediately gave instructions for all available Motor Ambulance cars of M.A.Cs to be placed at the disposal of the O/c 40 Divisional Advanced Dressing Station Flesquieres.

Evacuation was started immediately & when once clear, evacuation from the ADS Graincourt via this route went without a hitch.

Additional bearers were sent to ADS Graincourt consisting of one officer & a party from the 121 Works Coy, who rendered great assistance in bearing from the ADS to the horse ambulance wagon on the Graincourt Flesquieres Road.

1-30 pm. Capt P Gaffikin 136 Fd Amb arrived under instructions from ADMS 40 Division to clear Bourlon Wood with a party of bearers supplied from the personnel at ADS Graincourt. These were furnished the party proceeding en-route to the wood about 2pm.

10 pm. — A message arrived from Capt Gaffikin requesting further bearers. These were again supplied & at the same time instructions were sent as to the destination of his party, should the Division be relieved prior to his return.

26th
3 AM. — Relieved by an ambulance of the 62 Division, & handing over completed by 3-30 AM.

3-30 AM — Under instructions from ADMS 40th Division 'A' the personnel of 137 Field Ambulance proceeded to Hermies & thence later to Bertincourt.

135 Field Ambulance personnel proceeded to Trescault & the personnel of the 136 Field Ambulance together with all transport of the 3 Field Ambulances in use at Graincourt & Flesquieres proceeded to Trescault.

J. Minnell
Capt RAMC
for LIEUT. COLONEL
R.A.M.C.
COMMANDING 137 FIELD AMBULANCE

COMMITTEE FOR THE
MEDICAL HISTORY OF THE WAR
Date -1 FEB. 1918

No. 137 7.a.

SECRET

Army Form C. 2118.

VOL XIX 137th Field Ambulance
Dec 1917

WAR DIARY or INTELLIGENCE SUMMARY.
(Erase heading not required.)

Vol 19

Place	Date	Hour	Summary of Events and Information	Remarks and references to Appendices
LENS Sheet BAILLEULMONT	1/12/17	A.M. 7	Orders received to draw stretchers blankets & medical stores immediately to be taken by our	
			1st delivery point. Government to be ready to proceed to the same promptly. From	
			arranging with them as much medical equipment as many stretchers as possible	
		A.M. 9	Verbal message received from 121st Divl Bystle that above preparations were cancelled	
			and a warning order received to the effect the Bgde should be ready to move to	
			COURCELLES between 10 & 11 a.m.	
		P.M. 12.15	121st Divl Bgde when 156 Cpy No.7 received ord to Ambulance moving with	
			1st Brigade should be ready at 1 P.M. to proceed to HAMELINCOURT via BAILLEUVAL	
			BAGNEUX, BELLACOURT, RANSART, ADINFER, AYETTE & COURCELLES.	
HAMELINCOURT		P.M. 8.30	Ambulance reached HAMELINCOURT & learnt from O.C. 111th Field Ambulance	
			stationed there that it was to relieve 112th Field Ambulance at ERVILLERS	
ERVILLERS 5TC 1 Hrs ers B 12d 2.D.B		P.M.	Ambulance reached ERVILLERS	
	2/12/17	9.0	40th Division Routine Order No 414 of 1/12/17 received. "137th Field Ambulance will relieve	
		A.M. 11.0	112th Field Ambulance with Headquarters at ERVILLERS on the night of 1st December 1917"	
		NOON 12	Relief of Hd Qrs & Bearer party completed	

Army Form C. 2118.

WAR DIARY
or
INTELLIGENCE SUMMARY.
(Erase heading not required.)

137th Field Ambulance VOL XIX Dec 1917

Place	Date	Hour	Summary of Events and Information	Remarks and references to Appendices
STC 1 HDTN B.2.2 A/18.D.2.2 ERVILLERS	2/12/17	P.M 4.0	Relief of VI Corps Section SIGK (South) or ACHIET-LE-GRAND completed	
	3/12/17	A.M 10.30	Capt H.W. POWELL R.A.M.C. reported & assumed for duty & taken over duty as	
	8/12/17	A.M 7.8.0	Under instructions of ADMS 42d Division Kenan & Helper posts no to Sypercised &	
			to light Section of the line & adjust now to 136th Field Ambulance. Personnel at these posts being temporarily detached for duty with 136th Field Ambulance	
			Orders received from A.D.M.S. 42d Division to move all entrains from VI Corps Section SIGK ACHIET-LE-GRAND to H.Q. 2nd of O Division ERVILLERS	
	9/12/17	P.M 12.30	All entrains evacuated from ACHIET-LE-GRAND to ERVILLERS with help of 3rd MAC	
	10/12/17	Midnight 12.0	Party of 1 Officer & 21 OR's proceeded with 36 & 136 Fd Ambulances for temporary duty	
			Remainder of personnel & horses & transport & horse at this HQ Ambulance at ERVILLERS	
	M/12/17	A.M 2.0	1 NCO & 16 horses came returned from ACHIET-LE-GRAND to H.Q. 2nd of 68 CCS	
		P.M 3.0	Lieut F.E. MAGUIRE M.O. R.C. U.S.A. temporarily attached duty at H.Q. of CCS Capt H.W. POWELL proc to 135 Fd Amb 21st Brigade attached to 137 Field Amb M/s	

WAR DIARY
INTELLIGENCE SUMMARY

Army Form C. 2118.

Vol. XIX
137th Field Ambulance
Dec 1917

Place	Date	Hour	Summary of Events and Information	Remarks and references to Appendices
Sheet 57C 1/40000 B13 a 2.2 E.VILLERS	12/12/17	10 p.m.	Orders received from ADMS, 40th Division to send to Saputo one of 2 SBBrs, Reserve W.O.s & Stretchers per Squadron immediately to report for temporary duty with the Battalions of 121st Bgd.	
		11 p.m.	121st Bgd. Order No. 165. Copy No. 14 AND 12/12/17 received requiring the maintenance of the Battalions of that Brigade in times of "stand to" knowing so to "move" and dispersion of troops on receipt of order.	
	13/12/17	10 a.m.	Saputo return to Hd. Qrs. of Ambulance	
		2 p.m.	40th Div RAMC Order No. 46 Copy 2. 10 dated 13/12/17 received not accompanying work 137 Field Ambulance to be relieved on Dec 15th by the 5th ord Guards at CLONMEL FARRAGH Camp. (Sheet 57 C 11/40000 A50 d. 8. & Sheet 57 B 1/40000 S 26 c.s.a.) Orders to act as a reserve & supply Stretcher bearers & hands for the Brigade on the Picardie held in Reserve when necessary sent to Saputo 2 SBBrs. Bearers followed to report for temporary duty to W.O.s	
	14/12/17	10 a.m.	Visit from ADMS. 3rd Division & O.C. 9th Field Ambulance, The relieving Ambulance	
		8 p.m.	Capt. A.W. POWEL, detailed for temporary duty with 14th Army Brigade R.F.A.	

Army Form C. 2118.

WAR DIARY
or
INTELLIGENCE SUMMARY.
(Erase heading not required.)

Instructions regarding War Diaries and Intelligence Summaries are contained in F. S. Regs., Part II. and the Staff Manual respectively. Title pages will be prepared in manuscript.

Vol XIX
Dec 1917

13 of Field Ambulance

Place	Date	Hour	Summary of Events and Information	Remarks and references to Appendices
Sheet 57C 1/40000 B13 d 2.2 ERVILLERS	14/12/17	11.30 PM	Instructions received from 131st Inf Bde HQrs in the word "READINESS"	
			by telephone to Sergt Gaze with precis of duty for unit on receipt of similar	
			notice. Also Camp & Billeting Instructions.	
	15/12/17	AM	Advanced party of Ambulance + Regt of Field Ambulance	
		PM	Present SO+ m VI Corps Section billet now E with Field Ambulance	
			Unit moved into billets in CLONMEL CAMP HAMELINCOURT	
Sheet 57C 1/40000 A5 a 8.4 HAMELINCOURT		3 PM	Unit less detachment with 106th Field Ambulance arrived in CLONMEL CAMP HAMELINCOURT	
	19/12/17	9 AM	Capt P.T. O'Lukes temporarily detached as M.O. to 1st Devons R.E.	
	21/12/17		Lieut C.J. Buckley MO RCUSA reported sick to 20 CCS. Strength 136 Field Ambulance	
		4 PM	Lieut L.M. Sawdey MO RCUSA returned to duty from 1+C CCS	
	25/12/17	1:25 PM	40th Div RAMC No 47 Copy m/12 received. On 4th Inf 5 No 137 Civil Ambulance	
			(the case of the VI Corps Section of ERVILLERS (Sheet 57 C 1/40000 B13 d.2)	
			formed by 13 Field Ambulance	
	26/12/17	10.30 AM	Capt O.W. Howell temporarily detached for duty as M.O. 1/C 17 Welsh Regt	
		3.30 PM	Lieut D.A.H. Mais reported for duty. Posting between G.V.A. m complete strength	

Army Form C. 2118.

WAR DIARY
or
INTELLIGENCE SUMMARY. 137 Field Ambulance

Vol XIV
Dec 1917

(Erase heading not required.)

Place	Date	Hour	Summary of Events and Information	Remarks and references to Appendices
HAMELINCOURT	12/9/17	4.30 PM	Lieut Col N.E. Anneston RAMC evacuated sick to 49° CCS	
		5.0 PM	Advance party proceeded to ERVILLERS	
	22/12/17	12.30 AM	Capt J. McLennell RAMC attached from 17th Welsh Regt	
		8.0 AM	36 privates RAMC temporarily attached for duty with 36 Field Ambulance as stretcher bearers	
ERVILLERS		Noon 12	Relief of 4 / 1st Field Ambulance completed	
S9.d.57E			Remainder of unit arrived from HAMELINCOURT	
& 19.d.2.5		7 PM	Capt P.T. Endres RAMC attached February from ground RE's	
		8.45 PM	Lieut D.H.H. Morse RAMC proceed to U.K.	
			4 O.R's were evacuated to CCS by 13th Field Ambulance (two from Coy were attached suffering from shell-gas (wounds) on 13/12/17	

J. Mitchell
CAPTAIN R.A.M.C.
for Commanding 137 Field Ambulance

No. 157 7.0.

COMMITTEE FOR THE
...CAL HISTORY...
Date -4 MAR. 1918

SECRET   Army Form C. 2118.

WAR DIARY
or
INTELLIGENCE SUMMARY.

No 134 FIELD AMBULANCE

January 1918   Vol ~~XX~~

(Erase heading not required.)

WD 26

Place	Date	Hour	Summary of Events and Information	Remarks and references to Appendices
ERVILLERS (Sh 51e 4000) (C.3.d 2.2)	1/1/18		G.O.C. 40% Division visited the unit	
	2/1/18		19 OR Reinforcement arrived for duty. Lieut R.M. EUBANKS M.O.R.C. U.S.A. returned to duty from 45° CCS	
	4/1/18		Lieut L.M. SANKEY M.O.R.C. U.S.A. temporarily attached for duty to 45° CCS Lieut F.C. MAGUIRE returned from 20 CCS for duty	
	5/1/18		Under instructions from ADMS Lieut C.J. BUCKLEY M.O.R.C. U.S.A. was reinstated on the strength of the unit	
	6/1/18		Nil	
	7/1/18		Nil	
	8/1/18		Lieut F.C. MAGUIRE M.O.R.C. U.S.A was temporarily detached for duty as M.O. 1/c 13th YORKS BATTn	
	9/1/18		CAPT H.W. POWELL R.A.M.C. was temporarily attached for duty from No 135 F. Amb.	
	10/1/18		Nil	
	11/1/18		Nil	
	12/1/18		Nil	
	13/1/18		MAJOR (TEMP. LIEUT COL.) N.E. DUNKERTON D.S.O R.A.M.C. was struck off the strength under instructions from the A.D.M.S	

Army Form C. 2118.

WAR DIARY
or
INTELLIGENCE SUMMARY.

(Erase heading not required.)

JANUARY 1918
No 134 FIELD AMBULANCE
Vol XX

Place	Date	Hour	Summary of Events and Information	Remarks and references to Appendices
ERVILLERS	12/1/18		Nil.	
(Sh 57c 1 40,000 B13 d 2.2)	15/1/18		Nil.	
	16/1/18		Capt J.W. LINELL R.A.M.C. proceeded to U.K. on 14 days leave (17th to 31st)	W.M.F.HOPE
	17/1/18		Capt A.S. BEVERIDGE M.C. RAMC returned from leave from U.K. Capt WYCK-H McCULLAGH DSO MC RAMC arrived and assumed command of No 134 Field Amb	W.M.F.HOPE
	18/1/18		Capt A.S. BEVERIDGE MC RAMC was posted to No 135th Field Ambulance and struck off the strength accordingly. Capt H.W. POWELL RAMC was posted to this unit from No 135 Field Amb and taken on the strength	W.M.F.HOPE W.M.F.HOPE W.M.F.HOPE W.M.F.HOPE W.M.F.HOPE
	19/1/18		Nil.	
	20/1/18		Nil.	
	21/1/18		Nil.	
	22/1/18		Nil.	
	23/1/18		Lieut R.M. EUBANKS M.O.R.C. U.S.A. and Lieut F.E. MAGUIRE M.O.R.C. U.S.A. proceeded for a 3 days course to the Third Army School of Sanitation at ARRAS.	W.M.F.HOPE
	24/1/18		The D.M.S. Third Army inspected the Dressing Station and Corps Scabies Station worked by this unit.	W.M.F.HOPE

SECRET
Army Form C. 2118.

WAR DIARY
INTELLIGENCE SUMMARY

JANUARY 1918 No 184 FIELD AMBULANCE Vol XX

(Erase heading not required.)

Instructions regarding War Diaries and Intelligence Summaries are contained in F. S. Regs., Part II. and the Staff Manual respectively. Title pages will be prepared in manuscript.

Place	Date	Hour	Summary of Events and Information	Remarks and references to Appendices
ERVILLERS	25/1/18		Nil	
	26/1/18		Lieut EUBANKS M.O.R.C and Lieut MAGUIRE M.O.R.C. U.S.A returned for duty from Third Army School of Sanitation	
	27/1/18		Lieut EUBANKS M.O.R.C and Lieut MAGUIRE M.O.R.C proceeded on a 10 days Course to the VI Corps Medical School. Lieut C.J. BUCKLEY M.O.R.C. having being evacuated to the Base is struck off the strength from this date.	
	28/1/18		ERVILLERS was bombed during the night of 28/29. One O.R. RAMC was killed collecting a wounded man and 2 O.R. RAMC were wounded	
	29/1/18		Nil	
	30/1/18		Nil	
	31/1/18		Nil	

Whosh McGeloy
Lieut Colonel
Comdg 184 Field Amb
31/1/18

Army Form C. 2118.

WAR DIARY
or
INTELLIGENCE SUMMARY.

APPENDIX A

(Erase heading not required.)

Place	Date	Hour	Summary of Events and Information	Remarks and references to Appendices
			During the month of January 33 Officers and 1012 O.R. sick and wounded passed through the Dressing Station. Of these 139 were returned to duty. The Corps Scabies Station treated 398 cases of whom 243 were returned to duty. The Ambulance site was improved in that it was railed off and a motor Ambulance stand for 8 cars was made. The entrance and road was also improved. The personnel and patients huts were protected from aircraft by surrounding them with numerous parapets. The huts standing were also protected. A large Pack Store was made in a derelict building and the accommodation of the hospital thereby increased by 35 Jim wards were set aside and equipped as a Gas Treatment Centre. An officers scabies ward was also prepared. About 3000 men received ask trench foot treatment during the month and about 26,000 knoshs were bathed at the mry and Enillers baths.	

W.H. McCulloch
Cap'n R.a.m.c. (S.R.)
O.C. 134 F. Amb.

COMMITTEE FOR THE
MEDICAL HISTORY OF THE WAR.

Date −8 APR. 1918

No. 137. F.C.

SECRET

Army Form C. 2118.

WAR DIARY
INTELLIGENCE SUMMARY

No 134 Field Ambulance

February 1918   Vol XXI

Place	Date	Hour	Summary of Events and Information	Remarks and references to Appendices
ERVILLERS (Sh 57C H.000) (B13d22)	1/2/18		Capt J.W. LINNIELL R.A.M.C. returned from leave to U.K.	unknown
	2/2/18		Nil	unknown
	3/2/18		Nil	unknown
	4/2/18		Capt. H.W. POWELL R.A.M.C. proceeded on 14 days leave to U.K.	unknown
	5/2/18		Lieut EUBANKS M.O.R.C. and Lieut McGUIRE M.O.R.C. returned from VI Corps Medical School	unknown
	6/2/18		Lieut EUBANKS M.O.R.C. proceeded to 136 Field Ambulance for temporary duty. Capt P.G. FOULKES proceeded to 148 Brigade R.F.A. for temporary duty.	unknown
	7/2/18		Capt C.O'MALLY R.A.M.C. arrived from the Base and was taken on the strength. Capt A.H. LITTLE R.A.M.C. was posted to this unit from the 11/4 K.O.R.L's which was being disbanded.	unknown
	8/2/18		Lieut EMERSON M.O.R.C. and Lieut PEDRICK M.O.R.C. arrived for duty from the base and were taken on the strength. Capt A.H. LITTLE R.A.M.C. proceeded on leave to U.K.	unknown
	9/2/18		At 11.30 am the acting D.D.M.S. inspected the Dressing and Corps Scabies station. The Incipient Trench foot centre at MORY was closed.	unknown
	10/2/18		An advanced party of 1 Serjt. & 20 O.R. were posted at the new Billets in DURHAM LINES A. (Sh 57C S11a 36) (40000)	unknown
	11/2/18		1 N.C.O. and 25 O.R. proceeded to DURHAM LINES. 4 O.R. returned from H.Q. C.C.S. on being	unknown

Army Form C. 2118.

WAR DIARY

INTELLIGENCE SUMMARY.

February 1918 Vol XXI

No 134 FIELD AMBULANCE

SECRET

Instructions regarding War Diaries and Intelligence Summaries are contained in F. S. Regs., Part II. and the Staff Manual respectively. Title pages will be prepared in manuscript.

(Erase heading not required.)

Place	Date	Hour	Summary of Events and Information	Remarks and references to Appendices
			relieved by the 59th F.D. Baths at ERVILLERS and MORY were taken over by the 2nd/2nd North Midland Field Ambulance.	unixexnce
	12/2/18		1 N.C.O. & 23 Privates proceeded from DURHAM lines to A3 C.C.S. as a fatigue party for anti aircraft defence. Oct 1.30 p.m., after relief was complete and main Dressing Station and Corps Scabies Station was handed over, 134 F. Ambulance marched to Derham Lines near BOISLEUX ST MARC.	unixexnce
DURHAM LINES A	13/2/18		The 29 privates R.A.M.C. attached to 135 F. Amb. for Bearer duty rejoined H.Q.	unixexnce
(SL51 b	14/2/18		The C.O. attended a conference of Field Ambulance Commanders held by the A.D.M.S. It was decided that practically one Sections equipment was unnecessary	unixexnce
40600 S11036)	15/2/18		Captain C. O'MALLEY R.A.M.C. proceeded to the 21st Batt'n Middlesex Regt for duty and was struck off the strength	unixexnce
	16/2/18		Lieut F. C. MAGUIRE M.O.R.C. proceeded to 14th Argyll & Sutherland Highlanders for temporary duty	unixexnce
	18/2/18		Lieut C.F. LAUER M.O.R.C. was temporarily attached for duty from 136 F. Amb. Lieut Dr SAY REID RAMC proceeded to U.K. on 21 days Special leave	unixexnce
	19/2/18		Nil.	unixexnce
	20/2/18		Lieuts H.B. EMERSON and F.B. PEDRICK M.O.R.C. proceeded on a 3 day course to 8th Army Sanitation School	unixexnce

Army Form C. 2118.

WAR DIARY
or
INTELLIGENCE SUMMARY.
(Erase heading not required.)

Place	Date	Hour	Summary of Events and Information	Remarks and references to Appendices
DURHAM	21/2/18		Capt. R.G. FOULKES RAMC returned from duty with 178 Bgde	
LINES A	22/2/18		Capt. R.G. FOULKES RAMC proceeded for temporary duty to 145 CCS. Lieut L.M SANKEY MORC	
	23/2/18		admitted to hospital and struck off the strength	
			Lieuts EMERSON & PEDRICK MORC returned from Third Army Sanitation School. Lieut	
			LAUER MORC temporarily detached for duty with 45th Labour Company	
	24/2/18		Lieuts EMERSON & PEDRICK MORC proceeded to VI Corps School for a six days course of	
			instruction. Capt A.H LITTLE RAMC returned from leave from UK	
	25/2/18		NIL	
	26/2/18		NIL	
	27/2/18		Capt. H.W POWELL RAMC returned from leave to UK. Lieut F.C Maguire returned for duty	
	28/2/18		Lieut F.C Maguire proceeded on leave to Paris from 28/2/18 — 5/3/18. No 137 Field Ambulance	
			proceeded by march routes from Durham Lines A to BAILLEULMONT	

M.W.M.Cullen
Lieut Col RAMC
OC 137 F Amb

Army Form C. 2118.

WAR DIARY
or
INTELLIGENCE SUMMARY.

APPENDIX A

(Erase heading not required.)

Summary of Events and Information

The numbers trained at the Corps Schools ERNVILLERS from the 1st to 15th inclusive
on the 10th were 127 of whom 95 were attached to duty.
The total number of N.C.Os admitted for the month was 19 officers & 225 O.Rs
and of these 39 O.Rs were discharged to duty.

1 Surplus Luino A were prepared for ankau craft defence and the Pierway and
avenues of the huts repaired. Pits were dug in a similar road for
right hare standing of the tanks.
An Agricultural Plot No.167 was commenced.
Drill instruction under a Drill Sergt of the 1st Irish Guards was commenced at
the end of the month.
A small medical instruction card (eg attchd) was compiled and distributed to
all ranks RAMC

Lumsarculoh (?)
Lt Col. AMS (R)
OC 137 F Amb

0 grains or	} = 1 drachm (ʒi) or teaspoonful.	Castor Oil.	= Oleum Ricini
minims		Epsom Salts.	= Magnesium Sulphate
drachms	= 1 ounce (ʒi).		
o Ounces	= 1 pint (Oi).	Dental Caries	= Decayed Teeth
tablespoonful (ʒss)	= 2 desertspoonfuls (ʒiv)	Synovitis Knee	= "Water on Knee".
	= 4 tea - do -	Pyrexia	= Fever.

centimetres	= 2 inches.	T.D.S - T.I.D	= Thrice daily.
Kilo	= 2¼ lbs (roughly).	B.I.D.	= Twice " .
Litre	= 1¾ pints (-do-) 35ozs = 2 lbs	N.Y.D.	= Not yet diagnosed.
gramme	= 15½ grains.	D.A.H	= Disordered Action of Heart

Normal Pulse	= 72.	V.D.H	= Valvular disease of Heart.
" Temperature	= 98.4°F.	P.U.O	= Pyrexia of Unknown Origin.
" Respiration	= 15 to 18	I.C.T	= Inflammation of Connective Tissue.
cretion of Urine	= 50 ounces in One day.	N.A.D.	= No Appreciable disease. (Skin)
		B.F.	= Boracic fomentation
llar bone	= Clavicle.	H₂O₂.	= Hydrogen Peroxide
oulder Blade	= Scapula.	A.T.S.	= Antitetanic Serum.
.	= Humerus.		
re arm	= { Radius outside Ulna inside.	M↔D	= Medicine & full duty (not to attend.)
gh	= Femur.	D	= duty (has reported sick without a cause.)
g	= { Fibula outside Tibia inside	Attend A	= Full duty - attend daily.
ee Cap.	= Patella	" B	= Light duty - do - .
		" C	= Excused duty do - .

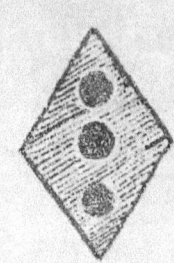 Nº 137

Field Ambulance
Medical Card.

12.16

140/2900

134 Field Ambulance.

COMMITTEE FOR THE
MEDICAL HISTORY OF THE WAR
Date 6 JUN 1918

SECRET MARCH 1918 Vol XXII Army Form C. 2118.

WAR DIARY
134 FIELD AMBULANCE
INTELLIGENCE SUMMARY.
(Erase heading not required.)

WA 22

Place	Date	Hour	Summary of Events and Information	Remarks and references to Appendices
BAILLEULMONT	1/3/18		CAPT R.G. FOULKES returned from temporary duty with 45 CCS	WAITANCE
	2/3/18		LIEUT H.B. EMERSON and LIEUT F.B. PEDRICK MORE USA returned from VI Corps Medical School	WAITANCE
	3/3/18		LIEUT H.B. EMERSON MORE was detailed for temporary duty with 10/11 R61 10 OR RAMC personnel as reinforcements. A School of Sanitation was organised under orders of the A.D.M.S. for the instruction of extra Sanitary men for the Division. 60 OR arrived for instruction	WAITANCE
	4/3/18		Nil	WAITANCE
	5/3/18		CAPT P.G. FOULKES RAMC was posted as MO i/c 40th Div. R.E.s	WAITANCE
	6/3/18		LIEUT F.E. MAGUIRE MORE returned from leave to Paris	WAITANCE
	7/3/18		Nil	WAITANCE
	8/3/18		Nil	WAITANCE
	9/3/18		Nil	WAITANCE
	10/3/18		Nil	WAITANCE
	11/3/18		3 OR arrived as reinforcements. One from 40th Div. Train and 2 from 29th Reserve Park ASC.	WAITANCE
DURHAM LINES	12/3/18		Unit marched from BAILLEULMONT to DURHAM LINES, leaving at 6.30 p.m. and arriving at 10.30 p.m. CAPT A.H. LEFFLIE RAMC was left behind in medical charge of details with one motor ambulance. 1 NCO and 2 OR were left in charge of a dump of unnecessary equipment	WAITANCE
Sh. 51B 40.00 S11a36				

SECRET MARCH 1918 Vol XXII

Army Form C. 2118.

WAR DIARY
or
INTELLIGENCE SUMMARY.

(Erase heading not required.)

134 FIELD AMBULANCE

Place	Date	Hour	Summary of Events and Information	Remarks and references to Appendices
Con U	6.3.18		LIEUT R.M. EUBANKS MORC returned from temporary duty with 136 Field Amb. Lieut J. Reed R.A.M.C. returned from leave U.K.	unknown
	13/3/18		Nil	unknown
	14/3/18		Nil	unknown
	15/3/18		At 6.55 am. orders arrived to fall in and be ready to move off. The Bearers were ready in 1hr 25min when orders arrived to say the previous order was cancelled. NCO taken on the strength from the Cyclists Base Depot	unknown
	16/3/18		Nil	unknown
	17/3/18		Nil	unknown
	18/3/18		Nil	unknown
	19/3/18		LIEUT R.M. EUBANKS MORC proceeded on 14 days leave U.K.	unknown
	20.3.18		Nil	unknown
	21.3.18		The 114th Brigade moved into support of 34th Div. around MENIN Hut. The Bearer Divn was under Captain J.W. Honnell RAMC and Lieut F.C. Maguire MORC followed the Brigade and formed an ADS in MENIN village at 10 p.m.	unknown
	22.3.18		At 12.30 am the 114th Brigade moved southwards and the Bearer Divn followed wounded were	

SECRET MARCH 1918 Vol XII   WAR DIARY
Army Form C. 2118.
137 FIELD AMBULANCE
INTELLIGENCE SUMMARY.
(Erase heading not required.)

Place	Date	Hour	Summary of Events and Information	Remarks and references to Appendices
ARMAGH CAMP S23a11 (S25IB to 40000) AYETTE		10.30 am	evacuated to ADSs at HAMELINCOURT (34th Div) and ERVILLERS (59th Div) HQrs 137 Field Ambulance moved from Sucrerie Luis A to Armagh Camp arriving at 10.30 am. At 4 pm the Dressing Station at ERVILLERS was evacuated by the 59th Div and the HQrs of 137 F.Amb. moved back to Ayette. Wounded were collected to the Dressing Station at Hamelincourt which was taken over as an ADS by the 2nd/1st Beaaros and evacuated to the MDS at Ayette.	
		7 pm	now by 135 F.Amb. Lt Col W.M.K.H. McCull of Riple was given command of the three Field Ambulances Bears Divisions Beaver Divisions of 136 Field Ambulance joined up with 137 F.Amb. at HAMELINCOURT. The Beaver Divisions of 135 F.Amb. moved to HQrs from ERVILLERS to the Sucrery (R1b.d.89) E of COURCELLES owing to the line retiring. Cars were posted as near as possible to all RAPs	ambulance
	23/3/18		An advanced post was formed on the HAMELINCOURT—ERVILLERS Road at its junction with the CROISS—BAPAUME Rd. Capt H.W. POWELL RAMC and Capt RAFFE'CAN RAMC remained in charge and evacuated from the 119th and 121st Brigades. Cars were sent as required 1000 yards up the ST LEGER and MORY Roads to the RAPs as required. The A.D.S. at HAMELINCOURT was shelled and 1 M.O was killed and 3 M.Os wounded. These belonged to the 31st Division	

SECRET MARCH 1918 Vol XXII

Army Form C. 2118.

WAR DIARY
or
INTELLIGENCE SUMMARY.

137 FIELD AMBULANCE

(Erase heading not required.)

Place	Date	Hour	Summary of Events and Information	Remarks and references to Appendices
	24/3/18		At 5 p.m. orders were received to move the A.D.S. southwards as the HAMELINCOURT - MOYENVILLE Road was not now in the 40th Divisional Area. The H.Qrs of the Bearer Divisions of 137 F.Amb and 136 F.Amb moved to the Quarry at COURCELLES arriving at 7.30 p.m. An advanced post was then formed in ERVILLERS on the ERVILLERS - GOMIECOURT Road and the wounded evacuated through COURCELLES to the M.D.S AYETTE as before. 1/2 135 F.A. Bearers evacuated wounded whilst 1/2 136 and 137 F.A. Bearers evacuated wounded down the BEAGNIES - GOMIECOURT Road while the ERVILLERS - GOMIECOURT Rd. The 42nd Division with Bearer Divisions arrived to relieve the 40th Division. The orders were cancelled owing to a further retirement on the right, and both Divisions remained in the line. The 162nd Bde. opened an A.D.S. in Gomiecourt. The post at ERVILLERS was heavily shelled and had to be temporarily withdrawn. HQrs moved from AYETTE to BUCQUOY at 1.30 a.m.	wounded
BUCQUOY	25/3/18		At 4.30 p.m. the Germans attacked and shelled all towns. The whole line fell back so that it was considered advisable to withdraw the A.D.S. W. of Courcelles. Capt. Powell Rome brought back all wounded to the Quarry which was cleared of its wounded. No Motor later Cars were despatched that night and all wounded in COURCELLES and Gomiecourt cleared. Capt. Powell Rome and Capt. LINNELL Rome remained on	

SECRET MARCH 1918 Vol XXII

Army Form C. 2118.

WAR DIARY
or
INTELLIGENCE SUMMARY.

(Erase heading not required.)

137 FIELD AMBULANCE

Instructions regarding War Diaries and Intelligence Summaries are contained in F. S. Regs., Part II. and the Staff Manual respectively. Title pages will be prepared in manuscript.

Place	Date	Hour	Summary of Events and Information	Remarks and references to Appendices
MONCHY-au-BOIS	26/3/18	1.30 am	duty EOL 1.30 am on the 26th. Orders having previously been received to rejoin H.Qrs which had moved to MONCHY AU BOIS and the Division having withdrawn the remainder of the Bearer Division marched to H.Qrs arriving at 8 am.	
POMMIER		8 am	At 8 am the Field Ambulance moved to POMMIER arriving at 11.30 am	WATERMARK
NOYELLEVILLE	27/3/18		The unit moved in accordance with Brigade Orders to NOYELLEVILLE arriving at 10 am It was then found that the orders had been changed and that the 121st Brigade had been detached to Sus ST LEGER. Unit moved at 12.15 pm and arrived at Sus ST LEGER at 5 p.m.	
Sus ST LEGER	28/3/18		Nil	WATERMARK
	29/3/18		Unit moved from Sus ST LEGER at 2.30 am and arrived at ORLENCOURT at 4 am	WATERMARK
ORLENCOURT	30/3/18	10.30 am	Personnel left ORLENCOURT at 10.30 am marched to TINQUES and entrained to the MERVILLE area arriving at DOULIEU at 10 pm. The transport moved at 11 am. with the Brigade Transport to LILLIERS	WATERMARK
DOULIEU	31/3/18	19 Qn	remained at DOULIEU. Advanced parties were sent to the A.D.S's of the 37th Division at BOIS GRENIER and CROIX-ESCORNEX. The transport moved into billets North of MERVILLE	WATERMARK

SECRET. MARCH 1918 Vol XXII

WAR DIARY
or
APPENDIX INTELLIGENCE SUMMARY.

134 FIELD AMBULANCE

Army Form C. 2118.

Place	Date	Hour	Summary of Events and Information	Remarks and references to Appendices
			Observations: The Bearer Divisions worked very efficiently during the fighting between the 21st and 26th March in spite of frequent moves and retirements on the part of the infantry. The casualties in this unit were 4 killed 9 wounded and two missing. The successful evacuation was largely due to good roads and the use of motor ambulances right up to the R.A.P.s.	
			Conclusions: (1) One Bearer cycle orderly should be attached 15 each Brigade H.Qrs to carry messages to the Bearer Division attached. This would obviate when Brigade H.Qrs move and short circuit messages from M.D.S. to A.D.S.s	
			(2) Each Bearer Division should have its H.Qrs close to Brigade H.Qrs so as to be better acquainted with proposed operations and in touch with the Battalions	
			(3) Each Bearer Division should be self contained with regard to rations, medical equipment and horsed transport. The latter should consist of 1 medical store limber, 1 G.S. Horsed Ambulance, and a water limber.	

M.N. McCulloch (?)
Lt. Col. R.A.M.C.

140/2900

134 Field Ambulance.

COMMITTEE FOR THE
MEDICAL HISTORY OF THE WAR
Date 6 JUN 1918

SECRET.

Army Form C. 2118.

WAR DIARY
or
INTELLIGENCE SUMMARY.

Nº 137 Field Ambulance

(Erase heading not required.)

Vol XXIII

April 1916

Va 23

Place	Date	Hour	Summary of Events and Information	Remarks and references to Appendices
Fort Rompu (H24 y 8 & 26)	1/4/16		137 F.A. HQrs marched from Y. Cava Gen Schol Dranken to Fort Rompu and took over from the 2/3rd Wessex Field Ambulance. The relief of the A.D.Ss at Bois Grenier (H24 d 62) and La Croix Lescornex (H26 c 93) was completed by 11am.	unknown
	2/4/16		Lieut R.R. MacGregor R.A.M.C. arrived for duty from the Base and was taken on the strength. Lieut H.B. Emerson M.O.R.C. was posted to A.D.S. at Croix Lescornex to assist Major Bowell R.A.M.C. Lieut F.C. Maguire M.O.R.C. was posted to A.D.S. at Bois Grenier to assist Capt Little R.A.M.C.	unknown
	3/4/16		The A.D.M.S. inspected both A.D.Ss and all R.A.Ps.	unknown
	4/4/16		Lieut S.B. Pedrien M.O.R.C. was posted permanently to 137 F.E. Surveys and struck off the strength.	unknown
	5/4/16		Nil	unknown
	6/4/16		Nil	unknown
	7/4/16		A.D.S. at Croix Lescornex was handed over to 136 F. Amb.	unknown
	8/4/16		A conference of O.C.s F. Ambulances was held at M.D.M.S's office to arrange a defense scheme in case of a hostile advance. Assistance was lent to 34th Div Ambulance at Erquinghem to evacuate heavy sick cases after. A.D.S. at Bois Grenier returned to Quex Trois Mouisons, one M.D. being left at Bois Grenier to follow up on the 9th. Lieut R.M. Eubanks M.O.R.C. returned from leave to U.K.	unknown

SECRET

Army Form C. 2118.

WAR DIARY
or
INTELLIGENCE SUMMARY.
(Erase heading not required.)

No 134 FIELD AMBULANCE

APRIL 1918

VOL XXIII

Instructions regarding War Diaries and Intelligence Summaries are contained in F. S. Regs., Part II. and the Staff Manual respectively. Title pages will be prepared in manuscript.

Place	Date	Hour	Summary of Events and Information	Remarks and references to Appendices
Q.H.Q	9.4.18		At 4:30 am a violent bombardment opened. Casualties from BAC ST MAUR, FLEURBAIX, query batteries as we applied and cars were sent in reply to telephone messages. At 11:30 am news arrived that the Germans had broken thro' on the right, so officers were sent to open an ADS at the wagon lines (A5.b central). FORT ROMPU and the PROLOW bridge. Beside it was heavily shelled. Cars were located in Road Ambulances Not the Canal. One M.O. and Bearer party arrived at 2pm from ADS BOIS GRENIER with news that the Germans had captured FLEURBAIX and that Capt LITTLE RAMC & Bearers were cut off. FORT ROMPU was Bombed and at 10 am R.A.P. 2 12th Suffolks. The Forde car at BOIS GRENIER escaped with wounded the R&D up twice. HQs arrived at DOULIEU MDS at 4 pm and marched thence to VIEUX BERQUIN, Bearer Q.Q. under MAJOR BOWELL RAMC remained near former wagon lines (A5.b central).	Innsisture
VIEUX BERQUIN	10.4.18		HQrs 134 F.A. opened a walking wounded post at VIEUX BERQUIN at 12 am and became an MDS at 12 noon when DOULIEU MDS was evacuated by 136 F.A. and received by 137 F.A. and 133 F.A. Bearer Co on ADS. The ADS under MAJOR POWELL RAMC moved at 10:30 am to A29 & 97 and at 12 noon it joined OPs of 136 F.A. at A21.58. At 6 pm it organised HQrs moving to an order given by D.O.C. 119" Brigade and a rapid advance by the enemy	Innsisture

SECRET

Army Form C. 2118.

WAR DIARY
or
INTELLIGENCE SUMMARY.
(Erase heading not required.)

APRIL 1918
Vol XXIII

No 134 FIELD AMBULANCE

Instructions regarding War Diaries and Intelligence Summaries are contained in F.S. Regs., Part II. and the Staff Manual respectively. Title pages will be prepared in manuscript.

Place	Date	Hour	Summary of Events and Information	Remarks and references to Appendices
	11.4.18		At 10.30 am the A.D.S. near Doulieu under Lieut M^cGRIGOR RAMIE retired to PRIMUS FARM (A42)	
			At 1 pm owing to a push further retirement on the part of the infantry was made. A new ADS was formed for the 3rd W^{ing} of LE VERRIER at the F21a central. PRIMUS Farm was evacuated by 134 F.A. at 7 pm. At 5 pm H.Qrs 134 Field Amb. moved to PRADELLES	
			The casualties treated at the M.D.S. VIEUX BERQUIN were 11 Officers and 131 O.R.	Weather
PRADELLES	12.4.18		Moved from PRADELLES to HONDEGHEM arriving at 4.30 am. One unit cyclist Moller to Composite Brigade H.Qrs as a Liaison for Brewer Division	Weather
	13.4.18		Brewer Division moved up at 12 noon but returned at 1.30 pm as not required. At 10 pm Lt Lieut EUBANKS M.O.R.C. was temporarily detailed for duty with (B.1) W.Fd.	Weather
ZUYTPEENE			moved to ZUYT PEENE arriving at 9.30 pm.	Weather
SCADERGRE (St OMER)	14.4.18		H.Qrs 134 Field Ambulance moved at 10 am to SCADERBURG arriving at 6 pm	Weather
	15.4.18		Nil	Weather
	16.4.18		1.6 O.R. Rank arrived as reinforcements. Is being to be equifed and from pack of a Composite Brigade	Weather
	17.4.18		42 O.R. Rank & 1 Sergeant Ambulance arrived from 135th and 136th F. Ambs.	Weather
	18.4.18		The Unit was inspected by the G.O.C. 41st Division	Weather
	19.4.18		Nil	Weather

SECRET

Army Form C. 2118.

WAR DIARY
or
INTELLIGENCE SUMMARY.

(Erase heading not required.)

APRIL 1918

No 134 FIELD AMBULANCE

Vol XXIII

Place	Date	Hour	Summary of Events and Information	Remarks and references to Appendices
	20.4.18		Nil	
	21.4.18		Unit left St MARTIN au LAERT area at 1.30 pm and arrived with the Composite Brigade near ZUYTPENE and were billeted at N24.a 8k24	Montague
	22.4.18		Nil	Montague
N24a (Sh 24)	23.4.18 5pm		Unit marched from N24a to billets at J.15.d.05 Sh 24 near OUDEZEELE	Montague
J15d05 (Sh 24)	24.4.18		Nil	Montague
	25.4.18		Nil	Montague
	26.4.18		Nil	Montague
	27.4.18		Nil	Montague
MENDINGHEM	28.4.18		Unit marched from OUDEZEELE Area at 3.30 and arrived in PROVEN area at 8pm. Park of 64 C.C.S. pitch at MENDINGHEM was taken over as billets and a rest station.	Montague
	29.4.18	At 1.30 pm	Lieut R.R. MACGREGOR with 1 B.O.R. and 2 Cars proceeded to GODE WAERSVELDE and took over a Dressing Station from the 33rd Division	Montague
	30.4.18		Nil	Montague

SECRET

Army Form C. 2118.

WAR DIARY
INTELLIGENCE SUMMARY.
(Erase heading not required.)

APRIL 1918   Vol XXIII   No 134 FIELD AMBULANCE

Place	Date	Hour	Summary of Events and Information	Remarks and references to Appendices

APPENDIX.

Main Dressing Station:- The cases passed thro' and held at the MDS during the month were:—

	Admitted		Evacuated			
	Sick	Wounded	Sick	Wounded	D.I.	Remained
Officers	6	—	8	—	—	—
OR	129	—	121	312	4	—
	8	316				

Bearer Operations from 9th to

At midnight 8/9th April Bearer HQrs & ADS were at Les Trois Tourettes (M22531 Sh.36) under Capt LITTLE RAMC with one officer, a squad and a car at BOIS GRENIER. There were squads at the RAP's & a relay post.—

At 4.15.am the Germans commenced their attack and Fort Rompu was opened as an ADS. in accordance with ADMS Defence Scheme. Casualties were received from the A.C. and the rough four lined, as well as from BAC ST. MAUR. Cases were evacuated to 136 FA

at SAILLY till 10 am and afterwards to MDS Doulieu until was opened by 139 FA

At 10 am. Horsed Ambulances appeared at Fort Rompu pontoon on a practise parade and were utilised to clear sitting cases from FORT ROMPU, Lts BOIS GRENIER party

Army Form C. 2118.

WAR DIARY
or
INTELLIGENCE SUMMARY.
(Erase heading not required.)

SECRET
APRIL 1918
Vol XXIII

No 137 FIELD AMBULANCE

Place	Date	Hour	Summary of Events and Information	Remarks and references to Appendices
			APPENDIX Continued	
			reported to HTrs. at 2 pm word was received that the ADS was cut off and that FLEURBAIX had been captured. The Field Surgeon moved to DOULIEU and the Bearer Div under MAJOR POWELL RAMC moved at 2.30 pm to the Transport Lines ASC central.	
			On 1.30 am on the 10th the ADS moved northward towards STEENWERK to A29.b.99 Lebreuvery to get in touch with 101 Brigade being to a retirement and being unable to get in touch with 101 Brigade except for its reserve Bttn. The ADS found up with that of 135 FA at X 3 a & b W of STEEN WERK A 29 b at noon. At 6 pm. both Bearer Divisions rejoined HTrs. at VIEUX BERQUIN at 6 pm under orders of G.O.E. 119 Brigade owing to a retirement. A reserve Bearer post at DOULIEU was kept open.	
			On the 11th the ADS at DOULIEU retired to PRINCE FARM at 9.30 am. It remained open till 6 am when owing to all no Acc cases being collected by the enforced posts of 135 FAS & 136 FAS at FAIR central it closed down and rejoined HTrs at PRADELLES.	
			O.C. 134 F. Amb. was Surgeonal Bearer O.C. during these operations.	

Hawkinswillers
Lt Col. R.A.M.C.
O.C. 137 Field Ambulance

14०/2983.

COMMITTEE FOR THE
MEDICAL HISTORY OF THE WAR
Date 9 JUL 1919

No. 1347. G.

SECRET

WAR DIARY
—or—
INTELLIGENCE SUMMARY.
(Erase heading not required.)

Army Form C. 2118.

MAY 1918

No 131 FIELD AMBULANCE

Vol XXIV

96 24

Place	Date	Hour	Summary of Events and Information	Remarks and references to Appendices
MENDINGHEM	1/5/18		Nil	
(EK 24) Ebd55	2/5/18		Capt H Rivers Pollock RAMC arrived for temporary duty, at 8 p.m. No 131 F. Amb. left Proven area for Oudezeele Area and encamped at J 15 d 05	
J 15 d 05 (SA 24)	3/5/18		Unit left Oudezeele Area for Kinderbeek (Hazebrouck SA 20.d.52.11)	
KINDERBEEK (Hazebrouck SA)	4/5/18		Lieuts Hamilton, Emerson Maguire More were posted to 33rd Divn for duty	
			Capt R Rivers Pollock RAMC was detailed to the 9th Bde for duty	
	5/5/18		Lieut MacGregor RAMC returned from duty at Godwaersvelde Dressing Station on being relieved by the 30th Divn. unit was posted to 33rd Divn. Lieut Brown N. Ok 3 pm this unit paraded with the 126th Bde for presentation of immediate rewards by the GOC Division. No 124 334 Pte Patterson JA RAMC (nursing) No Mb 178460 Pte Powell JWM, and No/2 182288 Pte Hall Pte RAMC A.S.E. M.T were awarded Military Medals	
	6/5/18		Lieut Lauer MORE was taken on the strength from the 13th Yorks and posted to the 1st Divn for duty	
	7/5/18		Capt F O H Goss RAMC and Capt D Crellin RAMC arrived for duty from the 12th Suffolks & 20th Middlesex	
	8/5/18		Capt F O H Goss RAMC was detailed for duty to the RB'n Corps	
	9/5/18		Nil	

Army Form C. 2118.

SECRET   MAY
WAR DIARY
or
INTELLIGENCE SUMMARY.
(Erase heading not required.)

1918 Vol XXIX   No 131 FIELD AMBULANCE

Place	Date	Hour	Summary of Events and Information	Remarks and references to Appendices
KINDERBEICK (cont)	10/5/18		Lieut R.M. EUBANKS MORC posted to 2/8th F Amb & struck off the strength	
	11/5/18		Major H.W. Powell & 10 OR proceeded to ISDOS (MOERIEL) to form a Car Post and assist MO of 16th Labour Group.	
			Nil.	
	12/5/18		Capt D. CRELLIN R.A.M.C. was posted to the 9th Div and struck off the strength.	
	13/5/18		Nil.	
	14/5/18		Nil.	
	15/6/18		Major J.W. LINNELL was temporarily detached for duty with 135 F/A Car Post.	
	16/5/18		Major J.W. LINNELL R.A.M.C. was awarded a MILITARY CROSS and W.S.1114 L/CPL VASEY & N/M ED. MOORE	
	17/5/18		Nil.	
	18/5/18		Nil.	
	19/5/18		No 78849 PTE. S. COX and 316236 PTE. G. CORLETT were awarded MILITARY MEDALS.	
	20/5/18		Nil.	
	21/5/18		3 NCOs & 50 OR commenced reporting daily to 183 TUNNELLING Co with 1 G.S. waggon for work on the LEDERZEELE LINE	
	28/5/18		Nil.	

SECRET MAY 1918

WAR DIARY
of
INTELLIGENCE SUMMARY.

Army Form C. 2118.

No 134 FIELD AMBULANCE

Vol XXIV

(Erase heading not required.)

Place	Date	Hour	Summary of Events and Information	Remarks and references to Appendices
	23/5/18		Nil	Winnezeele
	24/5/18		The medical defence scheme for C Coys of the WINNEZEELE - TERDEGHEM Line was submitted	Winnezeele
	25/5/18		Nil	Winnezeele
	26/5/18		Nil	Winnezeele
	27/5/18		Collecting Post of 136 FA at C30 b N.7 and 136 FA at O30 a 0.2 taken over	Winnezeele
	28/5/18		MAJOR BEVERIDGE M.C. R.A.M.C. and MAJOR McNEILSH R.A.M.C. with 139 O.R. another party of 135 F Amb were taken to strength of 136 F Amb. MAJOR BRUCE R.A.M.C. MAJOR CRAWFORD M.C. R.A.M.C. with 123 O.R. of 136 F Amb MAJOR BRUCE R.A.M.C. MAJOR BEVERIDGE M.C. R.A.M.C. proceeded with 136 F.A. Urging Cadre 136 F.A. Ear Post for duty MAJOR BRUCE R.A.M.C. was O.C. 136 F.A. on leave	Winnezeele
			16 A American Ind.	Winnezeele
	29/5/18		Nil	Winnezeele
	30/5/18		MAJOR BEVERIDGE M.C. R.A.M.C. proceeded with 136 O.R. of 135 F.A. and 104 O.R. of 136 F.A. to WARREN to entrain for OUTREAU and rejoin 135 & 136 F.A.	Winnezeele
	31/5/18		Nil	Winnezeele

J Col McCullagh
Lt Col
O.C. 134 F Amb.

14/3076

No. 1347a.

COMMITTEE FOR THE
MEDICAL HISTORY OF THE WAR
Date 7 AUG 1918

June 1918

SECRET

Army Form C. 2118.

WAR DIARY
INTELLIGENCE SUMMARY.

JUNE 1918   No 137 FIELD AMBULANCE

Vol XXV

(Erase heading not required.)

9A25

Place	Date	Hour	Summary of Events and Information	Remarks and references to Appendices
KINDERSELEK (Sh 24 24000) (G 33 c 88.)	1/6/18		Nil.	unimportant
	2/6/18		Major W.R.P. MCNEIGHT RAMC and Major H.W. BRUCE RAMC returned to 135 & 136 F Ambs respectively	unimportant
	3/6/18		10 OR RAMC returned to H.Q. from Krieken Post, the former Car Post of 135 F.Amb. No 75119 Pte MORRIS S. was sent to 9th Army School of Cookery for 3 weeks	unimportant
	4/6/18		Major J. CRAWFORD M.C. RAMC returned to 136 F.Amb for duty from these HQrs	unimportant
	5/6/18		Nil	unimportant
	6/6/18		The Rev. P. KERR C.F. (R.C) with his servant was attached to the unit for duty	unimportant
	7/6/18		Nil.	unimportant
	8/6/18		Nil.	unimportant
	9/6/18		Nil.	unimportant
	10/6/18		Nil.	unimportant
	11/6/18		Major J.W. LINNELL M.C. RAMC with 11 OR RAMC and 3 OR ASC MT and MAJOR H.W. POWELL RAMC with 10 OR RAMC and 3 OR ASC MT rejoined HQrs from duty at Collecting Posts	unimportant
	12/6/18		MAJOR H.W. POWELL RAMC evacuated sick to CCS	unimportant
	13/6/18		Capt C.K. CARROLL RAMC was posted to unit for duty and taken on the strength	unimportant

SECRET JUNE 1918

WAR DIARY
INTELLIGENCE SUMMARY
(Erase heading not required.)

Army Form C. 2118.

No 137 FIELD AMBULANCE
Vol XXV

Place	Date	Hour	Summary of Events and Information	Remarks and references to Appendices
	14/6/18		Capt C.K. CARROL M.C. RAMC proceeded for duty to No 15th Genl Bn. K.O.Y.L.I.	Inviroze
	15/6/18		Capt J STIRLING-GILCHRIST RAMC joined the unit for duty	Inviroze
	16/6/18		Nil	
	17/6/18		Capt J STIRLING-GILCHRIST RAMC proceeded to the 134th Genl Batt N Staff Regt for duty	Inviroze
			1 D.M. Sergeant, 1 Staff Sergt and 1 Sergt proceeded to 5th, 66th and 31st Labour Groups for 5 days to act as instructors for Regimental Stretcher Bearers	
	18/6/18		1 N.C.O. with 1 Horsed Ambulance was attached to 121st Brigade & NCOs in Lazaret to evacuate sick	Inviroze
	19/6/18		Nil	Inviroze
	20/6/18		Nil	Inviroze
	21/6/18		Nil	Inviroze
	22/6/18		Nil	Inviroze
C.8637 (Sqt 36A)	23/6/18		Unit moved to C.8.6.34 (Sqt 36A) near SERCUS Bourne KINDERBEEK at 15 Kms and arriving at 3.45 pm. The Ambulance continued to collect sick for the three Brigades	
	24/6/18		Nil	Inviroze
	25/6/18		1 O.R. RAMC returned from a 3 weeks course at the 2nd Army School of Cookery	Inviroze

WAR DIARY or INTELLIGENCE SUMMARY.

Army Form C. 2118.

SECRET

134 FIELD AMBULANCE

JUNE 1918 Vol XXV

Place	Date	Hour	Summary of Events and Information	Remarks and references to Appendices
			TEMP. MAJOR J.W. McINTOSH R.A.M.C.(T), CAPT B. ALLINSON R.A.M.C. (T) and CAPT L. WALTON R.A.M.C (T.C) arrived first duty from the Base Division and were taken on the strength	manuscript
	26/6/18		Collection of sick from the 121 Brigade only carried out as 135 F.A & 136 F.A. covered the collection of their respective Brigades	
			CAPT W.E. GIBLIN M.C. R.A.M.C (T.C) arrived for duty from the 89th Bn and was taken on the strength. The 2 No 5 M.A.C. Cars returned to their unit.	manuscript
	27/6/18		Nil	manuscript
	28/6/18		A.D.M.S. held a conference of all M.O.s of the Division at H.Q 136 F.A. Unit moved from Jerous and marching at 8 A.M. and arrived at 1st Cairo W.W.C. Station at	
M22a.3.4. (Sh.27)			T.7.22a 3.4. The Hospital was taken over from 135 F.A.	manuscript
	29/6/18		CAPT L. WALTON R.A.M.C proceeded for duty to the 93rd Cheshire Regt (Garrison Batt) and was struck off the strength. CAPT W.E. GIBLIN R.A.M.C proceeded to 1/2 N. STAFFORDSHIRE Regt and was struck off the strength	manuscript
	30/6/18		Nil	manuscript

J.W. McIntosh (SR)
Lt Col R.A.M.C
OC 134 F.A.

WAR DIARY or INTELLIGENCE SUMMARY

SECRET   JUNE 1916   APPENDIX

Army Form C. 2118.

Vol XXV   134 FIELD AMBULANCE

Summary of Events and Information

During the month of June except for a few days the men were the only influenza in the Division. All sick were collected by it.

Owing to the prevalence of Influenza 17 Officers and 661 OR passed thro' this unit. Of these 183 OR were treated and returned to duty.

In the unit 2 Officers and 60 OR were taken ill with influenza in the space of 8 days. The disease in it's sudden onset with headache, fever, pain in the back and limbs, weakness and prostration, loss of appetite and occasional vomiting. Its duration 48 hours. Complete recovery of appetite, taste and strength did not occur for 4 to 8 days after the temperature became normal. The treatment was Aspirin and palliative.

Senior N.C.O.s were sent as instructors in stretcher bearing to Labour Groups.

A body of recruited bearers from the Garrison Battn in the Base received instruction in stretcher bearing and 1st aid at this HQrs for 3 days. Others were trained in war gas duties and in Sanitation.

Lawrence-Castle Lucas (?)
Lt Col RAMC
OC 134 F. Amb.

144/3131

134t F.A.

SECRET   JULY 1918   **WAR DIARY**   Army Form C. 2118.

INTELLIGENCE SUMMARY.
(Erase heading not required.)

No 134 FIELD AMBULANCE   VOL XXVI

WO 26

Place	Date	Hour	Summary of Events and Information	Remarks and references to Appendices
T22a.3.4. (Sh 27)	1/7/18	Nil		wancourt
	2/7/18	Nil		wancourt
	3/7/18		Major H.W. Power R.A.M.C. returned to duty from C.C.S. In the King's Birthday Honours Gazette 1918, the undermentioned men obtained awards:— 61953 L/Serjt. R.S. Fitzgibbon R.E. was awarded the meritorious service medal 71956 a/Serjt. S.W. Briggs " " " " " a mention 71738 Pte. L/Cpl. Hacking T " " " "	
	4/7/18	Nil		wancourt
	5/7/18	Nil		wancourt
	6/7/18	Nil		wancourt
	7/7/18	Nil		wancourt
	8/7/18	Nil		wancourt
	9/7/18		Temp. Major J.W. McIntosh R.A.M.C. (T.F.) proceeded to 56 C.C.S. for temporary duty was taken on the strength of 59 C.C.S. and was struck off the strength of this unit. Lieut. H. Carr M.O.R.C., Lieut. A.B. Mills M.O.R.C. and Lieut A.D. Tyree M.O.R.C. reported for duty and were taken on the strength.	wancourt

SECRET JULY 1918

WAR DIARY
INTELLIGENCE SUMMARY.

Vol XXVI   No 134 FIELD AMBULANCE

Army Form C. 2118.

Place	Date	Hour	Summary of Events and Information	Remarks and references to Appendices
	10/7/18		LIEUT H. CARR M.O.R.C U.S.A. proceeded to the 94th F.Amb for duty and was struck off the strength.	
	11/7/18		Nil.	
	12/7/18		Nil.	
	13/7/18		Nil.	
	14/7/18		Nil.	
	15/7/18		Nil	
	16/7/18		Nil	
	17/7/18		Nil	
	18/7/18		Nil	
	19/7/18		One O.R. despatched to 83 General Hospital for duty	
	20/7/18		1 A.O.R. arrived per reinforcements	
	21/7/18		Nil	
	22/7/18		Nil	
	23/7/18		Nil	
	24/7/18		One O.R. A.S.C. M.T. despatched to England as candidate for Commission in R.A.F.	

Army Form C. 2118.

WAR DIARY
INTELLIGENCE SUMMARY.
(Erase heading not required.)

139 FIELD AMBULANCE

SECRET
JULY 1918
VOL XXVI

Place	Date	Hour	Summary of Events and Information	Remarks and references to Appendices
	25/7/18		The floors of all tents and marquees were covered by 1 foot and paraffin made to protect patients and personnel against bombs	aeroplane
	26/7/18		Nil	aeroplane
	27/7/18		Capt J.S. STEWART M.C. R.A.M.C. arrived for duty	aeroplane
	28/7/18		Nil	aeroplane
	29/7/18		Nil	aeroplane
	30/7/18		Nil	Nil
	31/7/18		Nil	Nil
				B
			Total of Officers admitted to Field Ambulance during month - 40 = Bir 6, 31st Bir 1, Corpo Ubropo 1. All were evacuated to CCS	
			Total of O.R's admitted to Field Ambulance during month - 445 = Bir 235, 166 Bir 1, 31st Bir 15, 49th Bir 1, 9th Bir 1, Corpo Ubropo 28, 5th Bir 1, Q Arms 149 were returned to duty	Nil

Maxwell May Rance
for O.C. 139th Field Ambulance

WAR DIARY
INTELLIGENCE SUMMARY

Army Form C. 2118.

SECRET

134 FIELD AMBULANCE

JULY 1918

Vol XXVI

Place	Date	Hour	Summary of Events and Information	Remarks and references to Appendices

APPENDIX.

During the month a class was held in ward work and nursing duties for those who had practical experience of the 16 candidates for examination were recommended for promotion to 2nd Class Nursing Orderlies.

A Batta Chiropodist class was held during the month. Two representatives were sent for training from each of the 4 Battns. These were given a 10-14 days course, examined and reported on to the R.M.O.

A class was also held for Regimental medical Orderlies. One or two were sent from each Battn in the Brigade and were replaced by R.A.M.C. orderlies from the unit till this course was completed.

A Dr. Medl. Sergeant and a Sanitary Sergt. were attached for 3 days to each Battn. M.O. to assist in the instruction of the regimental stretcher bearers and the sanitary men.

Owing to the great scarcity of water for ablution purposes a shaft was sunk by miners in the unit, after descending 35 and failing to find water the effort was abandoned.

LtCol McCulloch (GR)
Lt-Col R.A.M.C.

140/3200.

134" 4.0.

Aug 1918.

WAR DIARY
INTELLIGENCE SUMMARY

Army Form C. 2118.

137 Field Ambulance

Vol XXVII   Aug 1918

Place	Date	Hour	Summary of Events and Information	Remarks and references to Appendices
Sheet 27 H 40 a.a. T.32.a.3.d	1/8/18		Nil	ML
	2/8/18		Nil	ML
	3/8/18		Lieut A.D. TYREE, M.O.R.C. proceeded to 93 Fd Amb for temp: duty & instruction. Fire broke out in a hospital marquee caused by explosion of Primus Stove. Quickly extinguished with damage to tent alone. No patients injured & practically no equipment destroyed.	
	4/8/18		Lieut A.B. MILLS, M.O.R.C. proceeded for duty as M.O. i/c XV Corps Reinforcement Bn. (15th Royal Scots)	ML
	5/8/18		40th Divisional R.A.M.C. Sports held at Hd Qrs of 136th Fd. Amb.	ML
	6/8/18		Capt J.S. STEWART, M.C. R.A.M.C. proceeded for duty as M.O. i/c 10 K.O.S.B. & struck off the strength. 1 O.R. (NCO) admitted for duty from 136 Fd Amb. Regimental Court of Inquiry was held on origin of fire under instructions of A. Dir. of M. Svs.	
	7/8/18		1 NCO returned to duty from 64 CCS (Gas) on strength.	ML
	8/8/18		Nil	ML

9/R 27

WAR DIARY
INTELLIGENCE SUMMARY.
(Erase heading not required.)

Army Form C. 2118.

137 Field Ambulance

Secret Vol XVII

Aug 1918

Place	Date	Hour	Summary of Events and Information	Remarks and references to Appendices
	9/8/18		Nil	
	10/8/18		Nil	
	11/8/18		Nil	
	12/8/18		1 Private dispatched to Rouen for transfer to Infantry at his own request	
			Lieut A.B. MILLS M.O. R.C. returned to duty	
	13/8/18		1 Private transferred to 1/3rd W. Riding Fd Amb for duty	
	14/8/18		Lieut Col W. McK. McCullagh returned from leave	
	15/8/18		Nil	
	16/8/18		Nil	
	17/8/18		Nil	
	18/8/18		1 Staff Sergt, 1 Serg. and 2 Corporals arrived as reinforcements from the Base	
	19/8/18		1 Private dispatched to England as a cadet in the R.A.F.	
	20/8/18		Lieut A.B. MILLS M.O. R.C. and 25 O.R. proceeded to Musasy and took over No 1 XV Corps Walking Wounded Post.	
	21/8/18		1 NCO & file attached to 149 Sanitary Sect. for the construction of sanitary appliances	
	22/8/18		Nil	

Army Form C. 2118.

WAR DIARY
INTELLIGENCE SUMMARY.
(Erase heading not required.)

Title pages will be prepared in manuscript. August 1918 Vol XXVII 134 Field Ambulance

Place	Date	Hour	Summary of Events and Information	Remarks and references to Appendices
	23/8/18		An advanced party under CAPT B ALLINSON RAMC proceeded to 36 A/CS No 9 to the MDS of the 31st Division	unique
36A/CSaS9	24/8/18		Unit marched to CSa 59 and took over the MDS from the 93rd F.Amb. A medical Inspection Room at LE ROMARIN was also taken over	unique
	25/8/18		1 Staff RAMC proceeded to England as a Cadet. Lieut TYRIE MORE rejoined HQ fm 133rd F.Amb. He temporarily detached for duty with the John Major HAZEBROUK	unique
	26/8/18		MAJOR J.W. LINNELL M.C. RAMC proceeded to 14 sharp Base B.V.K. LIEUT A.B. MILLS and party rejoined HQ various periods over No1 X.C.WMR to 24 F.Amb. CAPT L.S. PILGRIM Dental Surgeon attached to this unit for duty with the Divison	unique
	27/8/18		An attack was made at 10.30 am by the 149th Brigade Kights N of NEUF BERQUIN The following casualties passed thro' the MDS in the 24 hrs following. Wounded Off 14 OR 174 B.W. 9 Gassed " 1 " 21 Nil	unique
	28/8/18		Nil	unique

Army Form C. 2118.

WAR DIARY
INTELLIGENCE SUMMARY

of 13th Field Ambulance

August 1918. Vol XXVII

Place	Date	Hour	Summary of Events and Information	Remarks and references to Appendices
	29/8/18		Nil	Appendix
	30/8/18		One Sergt. A.S.C. despatched to England for training in an Officer Cadet Unit	Appendix
	31/8/18	7.30 am	the unit moved to LA MOTTE 86A/D30 d09 and the M.D.S. was closed at C5a.59 (WALLON CAPPELLE) and opened skn the church at LA MOTTE at 9 am. Lieut A.D. TYRIE MORC moved a party was left to form a sick collecting post. The Bands moved to 136 F.A. at 6.30 pm and rejoined HQrs at LA MOTTE	Appendix

Appendix:- During the month the following cases passed thro' the unit. Sick officers 25, O.R. 335; wounded off 14, O.R. 268 including passed off 3 O.R. 68. of these H.Q.R. wounded and 41 O.R. sick were treated and returned to duty.

Mayor Cullen
Lt Col RAMC
OC 13 FA

Mayor Cullen
Lt Col RAMC
OC 13 FA

16/3259

137. Field Amb.

July 7. 1918

COMMITTEE FOR THE
MEDICAL HISTORY OF THE WAR
Date 9 NOV 1916

Army Form C. 2118.

WAR DIARY
or
INTELLIGENCE SUMMARY.
(Erase heading not required.)

135 FIELD AMBULANCE

SEPTEMBER 1918 VOL XXVIII

Place	Date	Hour	Summary of Events and Information	Remarks and references to Appendices
LA MOTTE (36 A/ D30 d09)	1/9/18		Unit detached to retired from Sem mega Hay brush. 29 Sanitary Section DMS office Sick Post at LE ROMARIN and the battle at WALLON CAPELLE. NCO proceeded for a course at X/ Corps Gas School	
	2/9/18		Jun O.R. to a – Army School of Cookery	
	3/9/18		M.D.S. with HQrs unit moved from LA MOTTE CHURCH to CAST FARM (E21 a 42) working parties from the unit continued to map the M.D.S. and make additional attacks to the M.D.S.	
	4/9/18			
	5/9/18		Nil	
	6/9/18		At 12 noon the M.D.S. became a D.R.S. which continued to be administered by this unit. M.A.C. cars were despatched 15 M.D.S (136 F.A.)	
	7/9/18		Forward area inspected.	
36/ A21 b28	8/9/18		A Bearer Subdivision and Lieut A.D. TYRE MORE under command of Major H.W. POWELL RAME proceeded to ADS at A24 d R1 and relieved 135 F.A. Bearer	
	9/9/18		HQrs of unit moved from CAST FARM at 8.30 am and established themselves at A21 b26. A sick collecting post was opened for the Brigade in Support	

WAR DIARY

Army Form C. 2118.

SECRET

Instructions regarding War Diaries and Intelligence Summaries are contained in F. S. Regs., Part II. and the Staff Manual respectively. Title pages will be prepared in manuscript.

INTELLIGENCE SUMMARY.

SEPTEMBER 1918
Vol. XXVIII

(Erase heading not required.)

134 FIELD AMBULANCE

Place	Date	Hour	Summary of Events and Information	Remarks and references to Appendices
	9/9/18	Nil		Initiate
	10/9/18	Nil		Initiate
	11/9/18		CAPT B. ALLINSON R.A.M.C. relieved MAJOR H.W. POWELL R.A.M.C. as O.C. Bearers. The latter proceeded to U.K. on Special Leave	Initiate
	12/9/18	Nil	MAJOR J.W. WINTER returned from leave	Initiate
	13/9/18		LIEUT P.R. SIMMONS R.A.M.C. evacuated for duty and taken on the strength accordingly	Initiate
	14/9/18	Nil		Initiate
	15/9/18		LIEUT A.D. TYREE M.O.R.C. and 1 N.C.O. proceeded to IV Corps Gas School for a course of instruction	Initiate
	16/9/18		4 O.R. sent to 40th Bn. Signalling School for a course of instruction	Initiate
	17/9/18	Nil		Initiate
	18/9/18		Unit moved to LE VERRIER (36A F.29 B.6.9) and took over M.D.S. from 136 F.B. The site at 36/A.21.6.2.2. was retained as a Car Post.	Initiate
	19/9/18	Nil		Initiate
	20/9/18		CAPT B.P. ALLINSON R.A.M.C. granted leave to France from 21/9/18 to 30/9/18	Initiate
	21/9/18		Two O.R. wounded gassed.	Initiate

SECRET

WAR DIARY
INTELLIGENCE SUMMARY

(Erase heading not required.)

Army Form C. 2118.

SEPTEMBER 1918 134 Field Ambulance
Vol XXVII

Place	Date	Hour	Summary of Events and Information	Remarks and references to Appendices
	22/9/18		Nil	
	23/9/18		One N.C.O. wounded and evacuated. Lieut A.D. TYRIEMORE and 1 N.C.O. returned for duty from Gas School. Unit moved to LA BRIELLE FARM 36H/L5a60 and opened up a new M.D.S.	
	24/9/18		Capt B. ROBERTSON R.A.M.C. reported arrival for duty from the 1/4 WORCESTER R(egt). Two O.R. returned from a Course at the School of Cookery	
	25/9/18		Capt B. HUNSON R.A.M.C. granted 14 days special leave to U.K.	
	26/9/18		Lieut Q.M. J. REID R.A.M.C. proceeded on 14 days leave to U.K.	
	27/9/18		Major H.W. POWELL R.A.M.C. returned from leave to U.K. In an attack W. of NIEPPE by the 25th Divn two the following wounded passed thro this A.D.S. Officers 5, O.R. 63, P.O.W. 3.	
	28/9/18		One O.R. wounded and at duty	
	29/9/18		Capt B. Robertson R.A.M.C. proceeded to BOULOGNE for duty.	
	30/9/18		A.D.S. moved from A24d21 to A9c82 (Sh 36) owing to the advance of the Left Brigade. A holding party was placed in STEEN WERCK Chateau grounds.	

Army Form C. 2118.

WAR DIARY
of
INTELLIGENCE SUMMARY.

(Erase heading not required.)

Place: American
1st Field Amb.
September 1918
Vol. XXVIII

Place	Date	Hour	Summary of Events and Information	Remarks and references to Appendices
			During the month 18 Officers and 185 O.R. were admitted sick and 114 Officers and 289 O.R. were admitted wounded. Of these 1 Officer and 63 O.R. were casualties owing to gas. In addition 5 Officers and 662 O.R. were transported by this unit to other E. Eds. of the Div. for admission. Since August 24th the unit moved six times during the stays at LAMOTTE CAST FARM, A21 b 23, and LaBRIELLE FARM enormous work was done to improve these places. Roofs were plated and made waterproof, approaches for cars were made, windows and doors had also to be made by the unit. Great days were also spent in draining and repairing the main roads in the locality. No 99205 Capt W.R Straw wounded in the abdomen died at C.C.S. One motor Ambulance was permanently disabled and two temporarily disabled by hostile shell fire.	

Lt Col W Culey (?)
Lt Col RAMC
O/C 13 Field Amb

14/3324

COMMITTEE FOR THE
MEDICAL HISTORY OF THE WAR
4 DEC 1913
Date

137th F.A.

Oct. 1918

SECRET

WAR DIARY
or
INTELLIGENCE SUMMARY.
(Erase heading not required.)

Army Form C. 2118.

137 Field Ambulance   No 2

OCTOBER 1918   Vol XXIX

Place	Date	Hour	Summary of Events and Information	Remarks and references to Appendices
LA GRIELLE FARM 36A L5a6a	1/10/18		An advanced party proceeded to STEENWERCK CHATEAU to prepare a new M.D.S. on the grounds (36/A12.3.5)	Appendix
STEENWERCK CHATEAU	2/10/18		Unit proceeded to STEENWERK CHATEAU and the M.D.S. was closed down and reopened there at 3.30 p.m.	Appendix
	3/10/18		An N.C.O. was detached to 224 Field Coy R.E. for the purpose of testing wells in ARMENTIERS. A.D.S. moved from NIEPPE 36/B9691 to ERQUINGHEM (H1B64)	Appendix
	4/10/18		Nil	Appendix
	5/10/18		Lieut A.D. TYRIE M.O.R.C. proceeded to 10th Battln K.O.S.B. for temporary duty. Capt HAWKS M.O.R.C. R.A.M.C. arrived for duty	Appendix
	6/10/18		Capt HAWKS warrant R.A.M.C. proceeded to 138 F.Amb for duty and was struck off the strength	Appendix
	7/10/18		M.D.S. handed over to 136 F.Amb who relieved that day from II Corps. Unit moved to LA HAYE FARM (36/1328.690)	Appendix
	8/10/18		Nil	Appendix
	9/10/18		Lieut P.R. SHANNON R.A.M.C. proceeded to H.E. Div. for duty and struck off the strength accordingly	Appendix

Army Form C. 2118.

WAR DIARY
or
INTELLIGENCE SUMMARY.
(Erase heading not required.)

SECRET
OCTOBER 1918   137 FIELD AMBULANCE
Vol LXXIX

Place	Date	Hour	Summary of Events and Information	Remarks and references to Appendices
	10/10/18		1 N.C.O. & Pte. proceeded to II Army Rest Camp for 14 days	Imgur "C"
	11/10/18		Capt. D. MEEK. R.A.M.C. arrived for duty and taken on the strength	Imgur "C"
	12/10/18		Lieut & QM. J. REID R.A.M.C. returned from leave to U.K	Imgur "C"
	13/10/18		Nil	Unknown
	14/10/18	At 0900	Unit opened a D.R.S. at LA HAYE FARM. At 1300 the Bearer Division was relieved in the line by Bearers of 135 F.Amb. and rejoined H.Qrs.	
			Lieut A.G. MILLMORE proceeded for temporary duty as M.O. i/c 23rd Lanc Fus.	Unknown
	15/10/18	At 0830	One officer and 35 O.R. proceeded to LA BRIELE FARM (36 A/I.28.b.60) and took over old D.R.S. with 119 patients from 135 F.Amb	Imgur spec
	16/10/18		Lieut S.F. BRENKLEY R.A.M.C. arrived for duty from the 61st Div. and taken on the strength	Imgur "C"
	17/10/18		The D.R.S. at LA BRIELE FARM was closed down at 21.00 hrs.	ambulance
WAMBRECHIES	18/10/18		Unit moved to WAMBRECHIES (36.A/N.2.B.49) at 16.15. Two F.Amb. just opened up an MDS and DRS combined	Unknown
	19/10/18		Nil	Unknown
	20/10/18		1 N.C.O. sent to XV Corps Gas School	Unknown
	21/10/18		Capt. ALLINSON R.A.M.C. returned from leave to U.K.	Unknown

Army Form C. 2118.

WAR DIARY
INTELLIGENCE SUMMARY

(Erase heading not required.)

SECRET
OCTOBER 1918
Vol XXIX

137 Field Ambulance

Place	Date	Hour	Summary of Events and Information	Remarks and references to Appendices
Cattaro	22/10/18		Nil	Unexpired
	23/10/18		Surgeon Lieut J.W. Pringle (R.N.V.R.) arrived for duty and taken on the strength	Unexpired
	24/10/18		Lieut. A.D. Tyree M.O.R.C. was posted as M.O. to the 10th N.O.S.I.B.'s permanently and struck off the strength. Capt D. Meek R.A.M.C. temporarily attached as M.O. i/c 10th Inv. Reg.	Unexpired
	25/10/18		Nil	Unexpired
	26/10/18		Nil	Unexpired
	27/10/18		One N.C.O. and 1 O.R. returned from II Army Rest Camp	Unexpired
	28/10/18		Nil	Unexpired
	29/10/18		Nil	Unexpired
	30/10/18		One Corporal R.A.M.C. appointed Acting Serg't. with pay. One Sgt. R.A.M.C. H.T. invalided to Cairo for a change. Corps: 17 Australian Veterinary F.R. Major J.W. Powell R.A.M.C. transferred sick to 11 C.C.S.	Unexpired
	31/10/18		D.R.S. closed down all cases being despatched to duty or to C.C.S.	Unexpired

(Signed) W.Clarke Colonel (R.C.)
R.C.L. Rome

Army Form C. 2118.

WAR DIARY
or
INTELLIGENCE SUMMARY.
(Erase heading not required.)

SECRET
APPENDIX
OCTOBER 1918
Vol XXIX

13th Field Ambulance

Place	Date	Hour	Summary of Events and Information	Remarks and references to Appendices
			During the month the following cases were admitted:— Sick 11 Officers & 161 OR	
			Wounded 14 Officers and 109 OR. Of these 1 Officer and 152 OR were killed	
			returned to duty.	
			During the last week of the month an outbreak of Influenza passed over 167,000.	
			R Cap OR. In this unit 1 Off and 5 OR have been affected. The epidemic is	
			more acute than that of July so that the cases have been more serious.	
			No more notable losses to Germans caused to brought however.	
			The personnel was cut off Division during the middle the week. Bulk of	
			Stonework Chateau. Nobin's Farm and infirmary quarters at Batta's Farm	
			filled in nine cases preparing C.K. and building of Wardrecques School	

Commanding Officer 13th
13th Field Ambulance

116/3491

COMMITTEE FOR THE
MEDICAL HISTORY OF THE WAR
17 JAN 1919
Date

1375 7.0

Nov 1918.

SECRET   Army Form C. 2118.

WAR DIARY
INTELLIGENCE SUMMARY.

Instructions regarding War Diaries and Intelligence Summaries are contained in F. S. Regs., Part II. and the Staff Manual respectively. Title pages will be prepared in manuscript.

November 1918   134 Field Ambulance
Vol XXX

(Erase heading not required.)

Place	Date	Hour	Summary of Events and Information	Remarks and references to Appendices
WAMBRECHIES	1/11/18		Lieut S^r. BREAKKY R.A.M.C. and Surg Lieut J.L. PRINGLE RN temporarily detached for duty with 135 F.A.M.B. who were running the D.R.S.	Weather
	2/11/18		One O.R. gassed, wounded and evacuated. Unit moved from WAMBRECHIES to CHATEAU LIONDERIE (37/14 2 N.E.) One W/ex Capt detached for duty to 103rd Div Reptn Camp	Weather
CHATEAU LIONDERIE	3/11/18		Nil.	Weather
	4/11/18		Nil.	Weather
	5/11/18		Nil.	Weather
	6/11/18		Nil.	Weather
	7/11/18		Nil.	Weather
	8/11/18		3 N.C.O.s & 25 O.R. detached for duty with 11 C.C.S. St ANDRé. Capt ALLINSON R.A.M.C. and 3 O.R. detailed to establish a Sick Post at KEERS for civilian sick owing to ravages of influenza in neighbourhood.	Weather
	9/11/18		Unit moved to PECQ (T1634) and Bearer Divisn under Major LINNELL M.C. R.A.M.C. forwarded forward to take over from Bearer Divn of 136 F.A. who were advancing across SCHELDT after the 119th Brigade	Weather
PECQ	10/11/18		A.D.S. established at OLPE T. owing to 15th Corps being cut out and the	Weather

WAR DIARY or INTELLIGENCE SUMMARY.

Army Form C. 2118.

134 FIELD AMBULANCE
NOVEMBER 1918
VOL XXX

Place	Date	Hour	Summary of Events and Information	Remarks and references to Appendices
			119th Brigade returning to MOUEN BAIX and CITE IN VERT area the Bearer Dvs required HDrs after establishing a Bearer and Car Post at C29 c 6.3.	
			CAPT ALLINSON R.A.M.C. was detailed to join Bearer Dvs and take over the medical case of Grand Civilcamp in MOUEN BAIX. These casualties were due to our gassed shelling in the night 6th/9th.	
			CAPT MEEK R.A.M.C. returned from duty with 1st WORCESTERS R. BATTN the Belgian 2 Infantry attached for duty from 135 F.A.	lancertrie
	11/11/18		Information of ARMISTICE arrived. Car Post closed down and 1 NCO and OR attached to 119th Brigade HQr at 34/J3 central. 4 OR returned from course of instruction at Signaling School. LIEUT A.B.MILLS MORC returned from duty with LIEUT CAMERONS.	lancertrie
	12/4/18		LIEUT A.B.MILLS and 3 OR detailed Breestraat Civilian Sick Post at LEERS.	hurserie
	13/11/18		NIL	luntsone
	14/11/18		One Belgian Interpreter returned to 135 F. Amb for duty.	luntsone
	15/11/18		One NCO A.V.C. AHA returned from course of instruction at Australian Veterinary Hospital. Unit work	
CROIX (ROUBAIX)	16/11/18		Unit moved from PEER to Croix Civilian Hospital at CROIX. Work to continue	

WAR DIARY

Army Form C. 2118.

SECRET

NOVEMBER 1918 INTELLIGENCE SUMMARY.

(Erase heading not required.)

VOL XXX

134 FIELD AMBULANCE

Place	Date	Hour	Summary of Events and Information	Remarks and references to Appendices
			40 beds were taken over for the use of the 119th Brigade. A curfew stopway	
	17/11/18		Practice with a daily attendance of 30 to 40 cases was taken up and also a waiting list of 50-60 cases.	
			Car detached for temporary duty with 20th M.A.C. Eight O.R. attached XV Corps	
	18/11/18		Thanksgiving Service at Ronkroix and a Ceremonial Parade of by the Service. Surgeon Lieut. J. PRINGLE R.N. returned from duty from 135 F.Amb. Unit attended a Divisional Ceremonial Parade of the R.A.M.C. held by Major General GUISE MOORES	
	19/11/18		A.M.S. D.M.S. II Army. Nil	
	20/11/18		One Sergeant R.A.M.C. attached for duty to A.D.M.S's office	
	21/11/18		Major H.W. POWELL R.A.M.C. discharged from 15 C.C.S. and granted 28 days leave to Paris. One O.R. from No 1 Company 40th Div Train attached for 10 days course of instruction	
	22/11/18		One BR A.S.C. M.T. and one large car despatched to 40th Div M.T. Company for transport. Surg. Lieut. J. PRINGLE (R.N.) detached for duty temporarily with 13th E. Lancs.	
	23/11/18		Nil	

Army Form C. 2118.

WAR DIARY
or
INTELLIGENCE SUMMARY.

(Erase heading not required.)

SECRET

13th FIELD AMBULANCE

NOVEMBER 1918
Vol XXX

Place	Date	Hour	Summary of Events and Information	Remarks and references to Appendices
	24/11/18		Capt. B. Allinson R.A.M.C. despatched for temporary duty with 15th K.O.Y.L.I.	Unwounded
	25/11/18		Nil	Unwounded
	26/11/18		One large ambulance car returned from temporary duty with 20th M.A.C.	Unwounded
	27/11/18		Nil	Unwounded
	28/11/18		One N.C.O attached to A.D.M.S's staff struck off strength from the 25-31/11/18. One L.D. L rose seconded to 51 M.V.S. One O.R. No 1 Company A.S.C. returned to unit	Unwounded
	29/11/18		One O.R. A.S.C. M.T. attached to unit from H.Q 3rd. Gd. A.S.C. M.T. Company and taken on strength. Lieut. Q.M. J. Reid R.A.M.C. despatched to England for a course of instruction in educational subjects at Trinity College Oxford.	Unwounded
	30/11/18		Major H.W. Powell R.A.M.C. returned from leave to Paris.	Unwounded

WM McCulley
Lt Col R.A.M.C.

WAR DIARY
INTELLIGENCE SUMMARY
(Erase heading not required.)

Army Form C. 2118.

APPENDIX.

134 FIELD AMBULANCE.

NOVEMBER R1918
Vol XX

The month's work was noteworthy for I Civilian Sick work, II Transport Assistance to Civilians,
III The Influenza Epidemic IV Education Scheme

I Civilian Sick work. At LEERS a post was formed and for 4 days from 5/00 to 16/0 hours
daily an M.O. attended sick there. At MOLEMBAIX for 3 days a M.O. attended sick and
gassed civilians amounting to about 60. Many of these had to be evacuated.
At LANNOY several civilian sick were seen daily for about 4 days. At CROIX for two
weeks two medical officers were detailed for civilian work. One MO at Croix sick so to 50
seriously ill civilians were attended in their homes from 9/00 to 16/30 the daily the
other attended 30 to 40 walking daily at the Dispensary in the Rue Emile Zola.
Rations and medical comforts were issued to all in need.
Dangerously ill were transported to Hospital by the units ambulances and at least 30
sick civilians were collected from places up to 20 miles distant and returned to their
homes.

II Transport Assistance to Civilians. At WAMBRECHIES horses and waggons were
supplied to civilians daily also at LINDERLIES where men of the unit assisted farmers in
ploughing as well as collecting their crops. At PECQ up to 6 teams of horses were

Army Form C. 2118.

WAR DIARY
INTELLIGENCE SUMMARY.

Opposition
131 FIELD AMBULANCE

SECRET
NOVEMBER 1918
Vol XXX

applied daily to farmers during the units stay there. As Czar in addition to one to two Red Potatoes being cut on Civilian work daily one to two fours were lent to Area Commandant for Sanitation work in the Town.

III Influenza Epidemic. There were 14 cases admitted sick with influenza from this unit of whom one died. About 30 men of the unit received their first dose of anti-influenza vaccine. All cases aboveground influenza were sent to 130 F.A. for treatment.

IV Education Scheme. Classes were formed for the men in French, Bookkeeping, Shorthand and Mathematics. Average attendance at first class about 35, for two weeks General Lectures were given each morning on subjects such as Brotherhood, Store Management, Motor Mechanics, National Health, British Africa, Farming &c

During the month there were 98 men treated and returned to duty, and 93 cases evacuated to CCS.

Munro Cutei 6(gm?)

147/2461

No 131/A/U

Oct 19/16

COMMITTEE FOR THE
MEDICAL HISTORY OF THE WAR
Date 6 MAR 1919

WAR DIARY
or
INTELLIGENCE SUMMARY.

Army Form C. 2118.

134 Field Ambulance

DECEMBER 1918

Vol 31

Place	Date	Hour	Summary of Events and Information	Remarks and references to Appendices
CROIX (M. ROUGE)	1/12/18		Major H.W. Powlin RAMC returned from leave to Paris	
	2/12/18		One O.R. sent on a 3 weeks course of Carpentry.	
	3/12/18		Nil.	
	4/12/18		Nil.	
	5/12/18		Nil	
	6/12/18		One large car returned from temporary duty with 135 F.A. Two G.S. wagons reported for duty to the Div Train.	
	7/12/18		Nil.	
	8/12/18		One large car again proceeded for temporary duty to 135 F. Amb.	
	9/12/18		Capt. M.E.K. Rome granted 14 days Special Leave to U.K. One O.R. reported for duty from XV Corps School and taken on the strength. One O.R. sent for a course in motor driving to 40th Aux. M.T. Workshops.	10ʰ & 24ᵗʰ ind.
	10/12/18		Lieut H.H. Parker RAMC reported for duty from 13ᵗʰ Royal Irish Fusiliers and was taken on the strength. Lieut J.L. Pringle R.N. returned from temporary duty with the 13ᵗʰ E. Lanes.	
	11/12/18		One NCO and 2 OR sent for duty with to 119ᵗʰ Brigade Medical Inspection Room.	

Army Form C. 2118.

WAR DIARY
or
INTELLIGENCE SUMMARY.
(Erase heading not required.)

SECRET
DECEMBER 1918
Vol XXI

134 Field Ambulance.

Place	Date	Hour	Summary of Events and Information	Remarks and references to Appendices
	12/12/18		CAPT DE CARGER R.A.M.C. reported for duty from the 13th E. Lancs. Taken in strength, despatched for duty with the 75th Labour Group and struck off the strength. LIEUT H.L. PARKER R.A.M.C. sent to 136 F.A. for temporary duty. Two minor cases "B.W.K." for demobilisation.	
	13/12/18		CAPT ALLINSON R.A.M.C. returned from temporary duty with 15 HQ 41i and posted 14 days Special Leave to U.K. 14th to 28th incl. One G.S. wagon sent to Sir Train for Temporary duty. Three minor cases sent to Base for demobilisation. One A.C.O. arrived for duty from Base. One G.S. wagon attached for Temporary duty with 136 F. Amb.	
	14/12/18		Nil.	
	15/12/18		Nil	
	16/12/18		One O.R. despatched to U.K. for demobilisation	
	17/12/18		One O.R. (miner) " " " Suff. LIEUT T.L. PRINGLE R.N. despatched to 178 Brigade R.F.A. for temporary duty	
	18/12/18		Nil.	
	19/12/18		Nil.	
	20/12/18		11 O.R. returned from temporary duty with 11 C.C.S.	

WAR DIARY
or INTELLIGENCE SUMMARY

SECRET
Army Form C. 2118.

DECEMBER 1916 Vol XXI

137 Field Ambulance

Place	Date	Hour	Summary of Events and Information	Remarks and references to Appendices
CROIX	21/12/16		Surg. Lieut J.L. PRINGLE R.N. returned from temporary duty with the 118 Brigade R.F.A.	wrwere
	22/12/16		Nil	ML
	23/12/16		1 O.R. taken on strength, discharged to duty from 11 C.C.S.	ML
	24/12/16		1 O.R. rejoined unit from 136 Fd Amb where he had been on temporary duty	ML
	25/12/16		Nil	ML
	26/12/16		Surg Lt. J.L. PRINGLE, R.N. detached T.U.K. for duty, returned at strength. Lieut A.D. TYRE M.O.R.C. U.S.A. reported aboard from 10 K.O.S.B. Lt Tim n Strength. Maj A.N. POWELL, R.A.M.C. transferred to Mulcahen Amre. Capt. Martin. Lieut Col WINCH & McCullagh D.S.O. M.C. proceeded on leave to UK (return 24/12–1/1/17). B.O.R's detailed for temporary duty to 72nd Infy Bde M.I.R. Lieut 19 L. PARKER proceeded to 135 Fd Amb for duty returns of strength	
	27/12/16		1 O.R. evacuated sick returns of strength from 12/12/16. 2.O.R. discharged to duty from 185 Fd Amt. 1 O.R. transferred to 26 Fd Amt taken on strength	ML
	28/12/16		Capt. D. MEEK R.A.M.C. returned from Special leave. 3 O.R.(nurses) & 1 O.R. (Sp. Service) Sect (G.S.) Corps Concentration Camp for Instruction to UK for demonstration	ML

Army Form C. 2118.

WAR DIARY
or
INTELLIGENCE SUMMARY.
(Erase heading not required.)

SECRET
137 Field Ambulance
DECEMBER 1918
Vol XXI

Place	Date	Hour	Summary of Events and Information	Remarks and references to Appendices
CROIX	28/12/18		1 H.D. Horse evacuated sick to 1st Strength	
	29/12/18		1 O.R. discharged to duty from 137 Fd Amb	
	30/12/18		1 O.R. admitted to 137 Fd Amb Sick	
			Capt B. ALLINSON, RAMC returned from special leave to U.K.	
			Lieut QM J. REID, RAMC returned from Course at Dieppe	
			Maxwell MacRae	
			Capt RAMC	
			for Lieut Col RAMC	
			O.C. 137 Fd Amb	

Army Form C. 2118.

WAR DIARY
or
INTELLIGENCE SUMMARY.
(Erase heading not required.)

137 Field Ambulance

DECEMBER Vol XXI

SECRET

Place	Date	Hour	Summary of Events and Information	Remarks and references to Appendices
			Appendix 1	
			During the month of December 1918, 114 cases were admitted to 137 Field Ambulance of these 37 were evacuated to C.C.S & 53 were returned to duty	
			Several lectures were given to the Units during the month. The average attendance at the Sick Parade in the Units was as follows:—	
			Church 21	
			Stafford 5	
			Hillmorton 4	
			The number of cases of Influenza occurring in the Units was nil. The number of men inoculated (light typhoid) vaccine up to date for Influenza was:—	
			2 doses 60	
			1 dose 5	
			2 M.O's were engaged daily in taking the Evening Sick Parade. The chief difficulty met with during the month was a deficiency of motor-transport, the average number of cars for duty being less than 3	
			[signed] M Munro Captain RAMC for O/C 137 Field Ambulance O.C. 137	

10/3440

40 JN
Box 2418

Jan. 137 + a

Jan. 90

Army Form C. 2118.

WAR DIARY
or
INTELLIGENCE SUMMARY.
(Erase heading not required.)

SECRET
JANUARY 1919
Vol XXXII

137 Gen Ambulance

9/8 3 2

Place	Date	Hour	Summary of Events and Information	Remarks and references to Appendices
CROIX (du ROUEN)	1/1/19		10.R. RAMC returned to duty from 140th Gen. Hosp. 1 O.R. RAMC attached temporarily (temporarily) to A.D.M.S 102 Hos	M
	2/1/19		10.R. RAMC (unanimously attached on duty) with 31 A.D.M Store	
			1 OR 8 SEES. H.C. despatched to U.K. for demobilisation	M
			1 O.R. R.A.M.C. discharged to duty from 107 Gen Mil. H.P.	M
	3/1/19		1 O.R. A.S.C. H.T. Southern Ambulance Car reported arrived for duty from 11 G.C.S	M
	4/1/19		2 OR's RAMC returned to duty from 11 C.C.S	
	5/1/19		Nil	
	6/1/19		1 O.R. A.S.C. H.T. discharged to duty from 35 Stat Amb. H.P.	M
			1 O.R. RAMC sick to Amb Amb 11 C.C.S.	M
			1 O.R. RAMC slightly wounded on duty to Duty in the Chay F	
			2 O.R's RAMC despatched to U.K. for demobilisation	
	7/1/19		1 O.R. RAMC despatched to U.K. for demobilisation	M
	8/1/19		4 O.R's RAMC despatched to U.K. for demobilisation	M
	9/1/19		4 O.R's RAMC LTo, Major J.W. Linnell M.C. R.A.M.C proceeded on 14 days leave to U.K. (11-25th)	Wimereux
	19/1/19		3 O.R. RAMC and 10 R. RAMC were being utilized whilst on Leave Book Stamb of Chateau of WIMEREUX	

Army Form C. 2118.

WAR DIARY
or
INTELLIGENCE SUMMARY.
(Erase heading not required.)

SECRET
JANUARY 1919
137 Field Ambulance
Vol XXXII

Instructions regarding War Diaries and Intelligence Summaries are contained in F. S. Regs., Part II. and the Staff Manual respectively. Title pages will be prepared in manuscript.

Place	Date	Hour	Summary of Events and Information	Remarks and references to Appendices
	1/1/19		1 O.R. despatched to U.K. for demobilisation	
	12/1/19		1 O.R. to U.K. for demobilisation. Lieut Col W.M. H. Mulch. M.D. R.A.M.C (B) returned from U.K.	
	13/1/19		1 O.R. to U.K. for demobilisation. 1 O.R. attached to A.D.M.S 20th Div. and struck off the strength.	
	14/1/19		1 O.R. returned from 2 course in Carpentry	
	15/1/19		1 O.R. demobilised on leave and struck off strength	
			Nil	
	16/1/19		Lieut A.B. Mills MOR C W&R returned from leave to U.K.	
	17/1/19		2 L.D. Horses stolen whilst attached to Hot Sy. Resection Camp and Struck off the strength accordingly.	
	18/1/19		2 O.R. despatched to U.K. for demobilisation	
	19/1/19		3 O.R. R.A.M.C and 1 O.R. 116 (P.B.) despatched to U.K. for demobilisation.	
	20/1/19		3 O.R. R.A.M.C and 1 O.R. R.A.S.C (M.T.) despatched to U.K. for demobilisation	
	21/1/19		1 O.R. R.A.M.C & 1 O.R. 8th January Reg. despatched 15 U.K. for demobilisation	
	22/1/19		2 O.R. R.A.M.C despatched to U.K. for demobilisation	
	23/1/19		Nil	
	24/1/19		1 O.R. temp. attached for duty with 237 Div. Employment Company as Cinema Operator	

Army Form C. 2118.

WAR DIARY
or
INTELLIGENCE SUMMARY.

(Erase heading not required.)

137 Field Amb.

JANUARY
Vol XXII

Place	Date	Hour	Summary of Events and Information	Remarks and references to Appendices
	25/1/19		1 male evacuated to Base	windsore
	26/1/19		Nil	windsore
	27/1/19		Major J.W. Kinnell M.C. R.A.M.C. returned from leave to U.K. Lieut A.D. Tyrie M.C. R.A.M.C. temporary detached for duty as M.O. i/c 119th Infantry Brigade	windsore
	28/1/19		Nil	windsore
	29/1/19		Lieut & QM. J. Reid R.A.M.C. promoted Captain with pay from 20/1/18.	windsore
	30/1/19		Nil	
	31/1/19		Capt B. Allinson R.A.M.C. temporary detached for duty with 136 F.Amb.	windsore
			Windsore Cully & the Ronnie (F)	
			During the month there were 182 cases admitted to hospital, 28 were sent to C.C.S., 15 to 136 F.A. and 54 to duty.	windsore Cully Jr
				Rose Ronnie

No. 137 Field Ambulance

14

SECRET

Army Form C. 2118.

WAR DIARY or INTELLIGENCE SUMMARY.

(Erase heading not required.)

FEBRUARY 1919   134 FIELD AMBULANCE

Vol XXXIII

Place	Date	Hour	Summary of Events and Information	Remarks and references to Appendices
CROIX	1/2/19	Nil		unimport.
[next] ROUBAIX	2/2/19		MAJOR H.W. POWELL RAMC returned from sick leave from CAP MARTIN	unimport.
	3/2/19		CAPT & QM. J. REID RAMC proceeded on a 15 days course in Sanitary Service to the Pasteur Institute LILLE	unimport.
	4/2/19	Nil		unimport.
	5/2/19	Nil		unimport.
	6/2/19	Nil		unimport.
	7/2/19	Nil		unimport.
	8/2/19		CAPT B. ALLINSON RAMC returned to unit from Temporary duty with 136 F.Amb	unimport.
	9/2/19		Lt Col W. MER. H. McCULLOCH proceeded to ADMS's office for temporary duty as ADMS	unimport.
	10/2/19	Nil		unimport.
	11/2/19	Nil		unimport.
	12/2/19	Nil		unimport.
	13/2/19	Nil		unimport.
	14/2/19		CAPT D. MEEK RAMC despatched to U.K. for demobilisation and struck off strength	unimport.
	15/2/19	Nil		unimport.

WAR DIARY
INTELLIGENCE SUMMARY.

(Erase heading not required.)

Army Form C. 2118.

Place: 134 FIELD AMBULANCE
FEBRUARY Vol XXVIII

Date	Hour	Summary of Events and Information	Remarks and references to Appendices
16/2/19		Major H.W. Powell R.A.M.C. assumed the duties of Acting DADMS in addition to those of Acting O.C. of this unit	
17/2/19		Nil.	
18/2/19		Capt. & Q.M. J.F. REID R.A.M.C. returned from V Army Sanitation School, LILLE	
19/2/19		Major H.W. Kinnell M.C. R.A.M.C. granted 10 days urgent leave to CALAIS	
20/2/19		Nil.	
21/2/19		Nil.	
22/2/19		Capt. Powell R.A.M.C. relinquishes his Acting Rank of Major from the 22nd/2/19	
23/2/19		Nil	
24/2/19		Major J.W. Kinnell M.C. R.A.M.C. returned from his leave	
25/2/19		Capt. H.W. Powell R.A.M.C. granted 14 days Special Leave to U.K.	
26/2/19		Major J.W. Kinnell M.C. R.A.M.C. granted 14 days Special Leave to U.K.	
27/2/19		The unit opened as a D.R.S. for the whole of the 40th Division	
28/2/19		Lieut A.B. Mills M.O.R.C. U.S.A. assumed duty as M.O. t/o 178 Brigade R.F.A. from the 22nd and struck off the strength from that date.	

SECRET   APPENDIX.
WAR DIARY   137 FIELD AMBULANCE
FEBRUARY 1919
Vol XXXIII

During the month the Unit occupied the Civil Hospital Croix and was open as an M.D.S. for the 119th Brigade. On the 24th it opened as a D.R.S. to the whole Division. There were 104 cases admitted, 69 were evacuated to C.C.S. and 29 to duty. Number of personnel despatched to U.K. for demobilization was 35 and in addition 7 were demobilised on leave.
Number of cases admitted to hospital from the unit was 6.
Two O.R.s enlisted for 4 years.
The Civilian Dispensary and outdoor practice was carried on all this the month. About 70 cases were seen daily by M.O.s of this unit and transport supplied to take cases to Civil Hospitals.

Wyman Cubitt Lt
R.A.M.C. R.F.N.R. (G.R.S.)

140/3031

17 JUL 1919

1371. 7.0.

Army Form C. 2118.

WAR DIARY
INTELLIGENCE SUMMARY.
(Erase heading not required)

137 Field Ambulance

MARCH 1919

Vol XXXIV

No 34

Place	Date	Hour	Summary of Events and Information	Remarks and references to Appendices
CROIX (in)	1/3/19		10 O.R. despatched to 11 C.C.S. for temporary duty	unimport
ROUBAIX	2/3/19		Nil	unimport
	3/3/19		Nil	unimport
	4/3/19		Nil	unimport
	5/3/19		Lieut A.D. TYRIE M.O.R.C. granted 5 days leave to Paris 5/3/19 — 10/3/19	unimport
	6/3/19		Nil	unimport
	7/3/19		Nil	unimport
	8/3/19		Lieut A.D. TYRIE M.O.R.C. returned from Paris leave	unimport
	9/3/19		One Amb. Car and 1 O.R. detailed for temporary duty with 148 Bde R.F.A.	unimport
	10/3/19		Nil	unimport
	11/3/19		Lieut A.D. TYRIE M.O.R.C. appointed Capt. from 17/2/19. Capt WOODROW R.A.M.C. reported arrival for duty from 181 Brigade R.F.A.	unimport
	12/3/19		Lieut Col. W. McK.H. McCULLAGH R.A.M.C. assumed duty of A.D.M.S 40th Div. vice Col. 14th M.P.H. R? who proceeded to U.K. for duty.	unimport
	13/3/19		Nil	unimport
	14/3/19		Nil	unimport

No. 137 FIELD AMBULANCE
M.H.H.
2/4/19

Army Form C. 2118.

WAR DIARY
or
INTELLIGENCE SUMMARY.
(Erase heading not required.)

13th Field Ambulance

Instructions regarding War Diaries and Intelligence Summaries are contained in F. S. Regs., Part II. and the Staff Manual respectively. Title pages will be prepared in manuscript.

SECRET
MARCH 1919
VOL XXXIV

Place	Date	Hour	Summary of Events and Information	Remarks and references to Appendices
	13/3/19		Nil	Appendix
	14/3/19		Nil	Appendix
	15/3/19		Nil	Appendix
	16/3/19		Capt A.D. TYREE MORE assumed duty as MO i/c 118 & 181 Portsalto RFA olso of 402nd S.B	Appendix
			D.g.e and P.O.W. Camp. he also took over OR taken on strength from 131 F.A	
	19/3/19		Lieut F.S. BREAKEY & 6 OR despatched to 5 army of Occupation (DMS 5 Army)	Appendix
			Capt J.B. WOODROW despatched for duty with army of Occupation (DMS 5 Army)	
	20/3/19		Nil	Appendix
	21/3/19		3 O.R. transferred to CCS	Appendix
	22/3/19		Nil	Appendix
	23/3/19		Nil	Appendix
	24/3/19		Nil	Appendix
	25/3/19		Lieut Col W.McK.H.McCULLOGH RAMC (SR) relinquished duty of ADMS 40th D. and	
			second S.M.O. 40th Division. Capt H.P. POWER RAMC admitted sick on leave to	
			No 30 General Hospital	Appendix
	26/3/19		Nil	Appendix

Army Form C. 2118.

WAR DIARY
or
INTELLIGENCE SUMMARY.
(Erase heading not required.)

139 Field Amb.

SECRET
MARCH 1919
Vol XXXIV

Place	Date	Hour	Summary of Events and Information	Remarks and references to Appendices
	27/3/19		Four vehicles HT returned to DADOS	Inverness
	28/3/19		Major J.W. Linnell M.C. R.A.M.C., Capt Powell R.A.M.C. and Capt B Allinson R.A.M.C. J Strength of boat out & placed on strength of DMS Nos Area	Inverness
			Nil	Inverness
	29/3/19		1 O.R. ASC N.C.T. arrived for duty	Inverness
	30/3/19		Nil	Inverness
	31/3/19			Inverness
			During the month there were 140 cases admitted of whom 117 were evacuated to CCS. and 13 returned to duty.	
			No. of personnel despatched to U.K. for demobilisation 17, demobilised on leave 1.	
				Inverness Cull R A?
				Lt Col RAMC

140/3740

17 JUL 1913

131/90

Army Form C. 2118.

WAR DIARY

INTELLIGENCE SUMMARY.
(Erase heading not required.)

SECRET
APRIL 1919
Vol. XXXV

137 Field Ambulance

WM 35

Place	Date	Hour	Summary of Events and Information	Remarks and references to Appendices
CROIX	1/4/19	Nil		improve
near ROUEN	2/4/19		2 O.R. P.B. Baker despatched to 900 Area Employment Company and struck off strength	improve
	2/4/19		Cpt/QM J REID R.A.M.C. despatched for month's holiday as Rqt. Officer with No.12 Ordnance Depot.	improve
	4/4/19	Nil		improve
	5/4/19		Capt POWELL R.A.M.C. discharged to duty from 30 General Hospital and taken on the strength and posted to that unit	improve
	6/4/19	Nil		improve
	7/4/19	Nil		improve
	8/4/19	Nil		improve
	9/4/19		Capt ATKINSON R.A.M.C. posted as O.C. 136 F.A.	improve
	10/4/19	Nil		improve
	11/4/19	Nil		improve
	12/4/19	Nil		improve
	13/4/19	Nil		improve
	14/4/19	Nil		improve

No. 137 FIELD AMBULANCE
No. M4/42
Date 2/5/19

Army Form C. 2118.

WAR DIARY
or
INTELLIGENCE SUMMARY.

(Erase heading not required.)

Army Form C. 2118.

Instructions regarding War Diaries and Intelligence Summaries are contained in F. S. Regs., Part II. and the Staff Manual respectively. Title pages will be prepared in manuscript.

SECRET
APRIL 1919
Vol XXXX

13th Field Ambulance

Place	Date	Hour	Summary of Events and Information	Remarks and references to Appendices
	15/4/19		Nil.	
	16/4/19		Nil.	
	17/4/19		Nil.	
	18/4/19		B.D.R. returned from temporary duty with 11 C.C.S.	
	19/4/19		Nil.	
	20/4/19		Nil.	
	21/4/19		Nil.	
	22/4/19		Nil.	
	23/4/19		Nil.	
	24/4/19		Capt A.D. TYREE M.O. 'C' despatched to St Quynn for demobilisation.	
	25/4/19		Nil.	
	26/4/19		Nil.	
	27/4/19		Nil.	
	28/4/19		Nil.	
	29/4/19		Nil.	

WAR DIARY or INTELLIGENCE SUMMARY

Army Form C. 2118.

SECRET
APRIL 1919
Vol XXV

131st Field Ambulance

Place	Date	Hour	Summary of Events and Information	Remarks and references to Appendices
	30/4/9	Nil	During the month lectures were given to the General Troops & Divisional Train, also 131 cases admitted to the Field Ambulance and of these 100 were evacuated to C.C.S. and 21 returned to duty. No. of personnel despatched to U.K. for demobilisation was 7, number demobilised on leave 14, and number granted leave 14.	

W. Atkinson Capt.
RAMC
O.C. 131 Field Amb
& SMO H.Q. Division

Army Form C. 2118.

WAR DIARY

INTELLIGENCE SUMMARY.

SECRET
MAY 1919
Vol XXXVI

134 Field Ambulance

(Erase heading not required.)

Place	Date	Hour	Summary of Events and Information	Remarks and references to Appendices
	17/5/19	Nil		Inverness
	18/5/19	Nil		Inverness
	19/5/19	Nil		Inverness
	20/5/19	Nil		Inverness
	21/5/19	Nil		Inverness
	22/5/19	Nil		Inverness
	23/5/19	Nil		Inverness
	24/5/19	Nil		Inverness
	25/5/19	MOR	RAEC H.T. being posted to 40th Div. Train	Inverness
	26/5/19	Nil		Inverness
	27/5/19	Nil		Inverness
	28/5/19	Nil		Inverness
	29/5/19	Nil		Inverness
	30/5/19		Colonel McCullough granted 14 days leave to UK	R.B
	31/5/19		2 P.B. Bahrin treated Cancer Sahin cant a struck off strength Rets	Rets
			W.E.	Rets

R.B Allinson
Capt RAMC for Lieut Colonel,
RAMC

SECRET

WAR DIARY
INTELLIGENCE SUMMARY
134 FIELD AMBULANCE

MAY 1919
Vol. XXXVI

Army Form C. 2118.

98 36

Place	Date	Hour	Summary of Events and Information	Remarks and references to Appendices
CROIX	1/5/19		Nil.	
M ROUGEUX	2/5/19		Nil.	
	3/5/19		Nil.	
	4/5/19		10 OR. A.S.C. (MT.) transferred to 40th Div. M.T. Coy	
	5/5/19		Nil.	
	6/5/19		1 OR R.A.S.C. (MT.) " " " "	
	7/5/19		Nil.	
	8/5/19		Nil.	
	9/5/19		Nil.	
	10/5/19		Nil.	
	11/5/19		Nil.	
	12/5/19		Nil.	
	13/5/19		Nil.	
	14/5/19		5 OR. R.A.S.C. H.T. transferred to 40th Div. Train	
	15/5/19		Nil.	
	16/5/19		Nil.	

No 134 Halle a/S Comee